Sixteen years spent pastoring a beloved but ~~profoundly wounded~~ Detroit neighborhood is simply one of the ~~~~ so deeply with this collection of essays. Br~~~~ let go of a "truncated" gospel that ignores ~~~~ reconciled. Ben Virgo's reminder that thos~~~~ not those who try hard—but those whose lives are rooted in the love of Christ. Danielle Strickland's call to an evil-fighting activism flowing from hearts that weep alongside the broken. And so much more! This volume compels us from the biblical text and the heart of Jesus to respond with passion to Dr. King's historic invitation: "If you can't fly, run; if you can't run, walk; if you can't walk, crawl; but by all means keep moving"—in solidarity with the God whose love moves him to see every son and daughter's pain and do all to heal us and set us free.

J. KEVIN BUTCHER, executive director of Rooted Ministries and author of *Free* and *Choose and Choose Again*

Angie Ward and the contributors of *The Least of These* make a passionate plea to Christians to examine our responsibility and action toward the most vulnerable in our society. The stories written in this critical volume open our eyes and ears to listen, learn, and love one another so that we can transform the world. I recommend this book to anyone who seeks to embody the good news of God's love.

GRACE JI-SUN KIM, professor of theology at Earlham School of Religion, author of over twenty-one books (most recently, *Invisible*), editor of *Keeping Hope Alive*, and host of *The Christian Century*'s *Madang* podcast

The collective wisdom of this book points us toward both hope and courage. I needed to be reminded that when we engage with the pain of our neighbors, we always find a God who is with us all; perhaps you do too. Highly recommend.

TIM SOERENS, author of *Everywhere You Look*

This book reminds me to see my own neediness in the mirror. The undocumented, the homeless, and many living in the shadows of unseenness—I could be them in a heartbeat; I am them. This book causes me to see the great need to match my doctrine with my service. This book makes me question if I am "showing my faith by my works" or just sitting in my castle with the drawbridge pulled up—until my day of need comes. Then who will help me? If we do not step up, who will? This book hurts where I need it. It's time to be real.

DR. ALEJANDRO MANDES, author of *Embracing the New Samaria* and executive director of EFCA's All People Initiative

The Least of These is an incredible compilation that focuses on the humanity of all people. The authors are leaders and practitioners who challenge us to know and do life with people who live at the margins. It even challenges the idea of margins to encounter each person as an equal part of the community.

REV. DR. LEROY BARBER, executive director of Neighborhood Economics and cofounder of The Voices Project

The authors of *The Least of These* thoughtfully invite us to consider how we see ourselves in relationship to our neighbors and push us to reconsider how our religious practices do not always align with how we ought to be in relationship with others. In a time when so many Christians are deconstructing their faith, these authors provide guideposts for those of us ready to start again and again.

KATHY KHANG, author of *Raise Your Voice*

The Least of These is a sacred gift to the church. The authors of these essays come together not just to exhort the church to love and draw near to God's preferred people but also to reveal how their relationships and experiences with those on the margins have transformed their own lives. This book is a beautiful invitation to draw near, love, and be changed.

KAREN GONZÁLEZ, author of *Beyond Welcome: Centering Immigrants in Our Christian Response to Immigration*

THE LEAST OF THESE

PRACTICING A FAITH WITHOUT MARGINS

ANGIE WARD, GENERAL EDITOR

NavPress

A NavPress resource published in alliance with Tyndale House Publishers

NavPress is the publishing ministry of The Navigators, an international Christian organization and leader in personal spiritual development. NavPress is committed to helping people grow spiritually and enjoy lives of meaning and hope through personal and group resources that are biblically rooted, culturally relevant, and highly practical.

For more information, visit NavPress.com.

The Least of These: Practicing a Faith without Margins

Copyright © 2023 by Angie Ward. All rights reserved.

A NavPress resource published in alliance with Tyndale House Publishers

NavPress and the NavPress logo are registered trademarks of NavPress, The Navigators, Colorado Springs, CO. *Tyndale* is a registered trademark of Tyndale House Ministries. Absence of ® in connection with marks of NavPress or other parties does not indicate an absence of registration of those marks.

The Team:
David Zimmerman, Publisher; Deborah Sáenz Gonzalez, Acquisitions Editor; Elizabeth Schroll, Copy Editor; Olivia Eldredge, Operations Manager; Barry Smith, Designer

Cover photograph of hands copyright © DamiWurtz/Pixabay.com. All rights reserved.

Author photo by Denver Seminary staff, copyright © 2021. All rights reserved.

Quotation from the poem "Is Justice Worth It?" is included with permission from Micah Bournes. All rights reserved.

The author is represented by the literary agency of WordServe Literary, wordserveliterary.com.

Some of the anecdotal illustrations in this book are true to life and are included with the permission of the persons involved. All other illustrations are composites of real situations, and any resemblance to people living or dead is purely coincidental.

For information about special discounts for bulk purchases, please contact Tyndale House Publishers at csresponse@tyndale.com, or call 1-855-277-9400.

ISBN 978-1-64158-417-3

Printed in the United States of America

29	28	27	26	25	24	23
7	6	5	4	3	2	1

CONTENTS

INTRODUCTION

NEARLY EVERY DAY, I take my dog on a walk around my neighborhood in my adopted city of Denver. In just a two-mile loop, I see so many needs. There's a man in a wheelchair struggling to cross the street before the traffic lights change. There is a single mother among a group of grocery-store coworkers, picketing for a better wage in frigid temperatures outside the store. There are the diverse riders of the public transportation system waiting at the bus stops on several corners along my route.

There are college students with Black Lives Matter signs displayed in the windows of their dorms and rental houses, and students of all colors, ethnicities, and sexual identities making their way to and from class, sporting events, and watering holes. There is a homeless family huddled under the minimal shelter of the side entry to a local church, the entirety of their possessions contained in a shopping cart, the young children trying to stay warm in ragged sleeping bags. I walk past the elementary school that serves students from low-income families just blocks from the well-resourced school that proudly displays banners announcing all their state and national awards for high achievement. There are several neighbors with mental illness, their porches and yards piled high with clutter. And there are refugee families eking out a living with government assistance and praying their kids have a chance for something better.

Just two miles. So many different people. So many needs. So many on the margins. So many dividing lines. Honestly, it's often overwhelming. I'm tempted to just return home, shut my front door, and insulate myself. After all, where would I start? Who needs my assistance the most? And what, really, can I do? What can I give? Money? Time? My means, while greater than many around me, still seem so meager, so pathetically inadequate. Still, it seems I should do *something*. What is my personal responsibility? And what is the role of my church, of *the* church?

In this third entry in the Kingdom Conversations series, we wrestle with these difficult issues and questions. We know that in a fallen and broken world there will always be pain and poverty, sickness and sadness. Yet as followers of Christ we are called to bring hope and healing to those who hurt, and there ought not be margins in the Kingdom of God. What, therefore, is our responsibility to alleviate suffering and promote flourishing this side of eternity? With so many needs everywhere we look, where do we start? And what can we learn from those we deem as less fortunate than ourselves, but who in fact may hold the keys to the Kingdom of God?

I am delighted with and humbled by the voices we have

curated for this particular conversation. Each of the contributors in this book has personal experience with, passion for, and proximity to the pressing needs around us. They challenge and help each and all of us be better prepared to love and serve those whom the world often neglects.

Lisa Rodriguez-Watson opens by asking, "Who Is My Neighbor?," pointing out our tendency to distance ourselves from those in need and reminding us that by serving the least of these, we serve our Savior himself. David Hionides follows with an overview of the theology of the *imago Dei*—the image of God—and of human dignity. What does it mean for those on either side of human-made margins that *all* human beings bear the image of their creator?

From there, Ben Virgo takes us on a historical journey, using lessons from English history to show how ordinary people have ministered extraordinary, world-changing compassion in Jesus' name. Next, Dennis R. Edwards digs into a comprehensive examination of what the Scriptures teach about social justice, while Brandon Washington reminds us that social justice is not merely one outworking of the gospel; it is central to the gospel message.

Jonathan ("Pastah J") Brooks helps us turn the corner from theory and theology to practice, painting a picture of how compassion is developed through proximity and personal relationship. Daniel Aaron Harris then lays out a practical theology of a multi-ability church in which all women and men, regardless of ability or status, are created, called, connected, and commissioned.

Danielle Strickland calls us to engage the needs of the world, first through lament, and then by replacing lies with truth, fear with love, and separation with connection. Aubrey Sampson extends the call to the church, exhorting the body of Christ to serve as communities of glad hope bringers. Finally, Christiana Rice reminds us of our consolation in the hope of Christ, our deliverer.

As disciples of Christ, may we never forget, never, never turn away, never shirk responsibility to minister compassion and justice in the name of Jesus.

Angie Ward
GENERAL EDITOR

1

WHO IS MY NEIGHBOR?

Lisa Rodriguez-Watson

"MY NAME IS JERRY," he said with a strong southern Louisiana accent, "but most people call me Junior." His smile was genuine, almost childlike, and bore the truth of decades of neglect. "My name is Lisa," I said as we shook hands on my front porch. Junior's aged, wiry frame and gentle demeanor were disarming. He and I went quickly from strangers to neighbors. "Do you have any work for me?" he inquired. "I can sweep your porch and sidewalk," he continued. "No, Junior, I think the porch and sidewalk are okay today," I responded with what felt like a noticeable lack of confidence. "Well, that's okay, Ms. Lisa. I'll be back again soon. I just was gonna run to the store and get some Buglers. It's nice to know you. I'll see you again." Junior rode off contentedly on his bike, while I remained curious and cautious on my porch.

Junior was one of my first and best teachers of loving my neighbor. At the time, I was living in downtown Fresno directing an urban program for InterVarsity Christian Fellowship. Junior was well known and loved by the many cycles of students and interns who came through the program. Multiple times a week, Junior would come asking for work and money. Honestly, I often tired of his impromptu knocks at my door, which felt like disruptions to the important work I had to do of training students to be ministers in the inner city and writing fundraising letters to donors.

One day, still early in my time there on L Street in downtown Fresno, I saw Junior riding up on his bicycle and stepping onto the porch. It was just after Thanksgiving, so even though I was busy with my ministry tasks, I was ready to generously offer the leftovers I had in the fridge and send him on his way. When Junior knocked on the door, I answered and we exchanged greetings. Instead of asking for food or money, as was his custom, he made a very unusual request. "Do you have a razor?" Perplexed at his unique request, I must have stuttered momentarily. "Uh, a razor? Like to shave with?" I muttered. "Yes, a razor for shaving," he kindly responded.

What about the abundance of food I was ready to give? Why wasn't he asking for what *I* wanted to share? Why my razor? I had kind of splurged and gotten a nice one, and I didn't particularly feel like sharing it. All these thoughts were on a collision course with the passage I had read from James earlier that morning:

> Listen, my dear brothers and sisters: Has not God chosen those who are poor in the eyes of the world to be rich in faith and to inherit the kingdom he promised those who love him? . . .
>
> If you really keep the royal law found in Scripture, "Love your neighbor as yourself," you are doing right. . . .
>
> What good is it, my brothers and sisters, if someone claims to have faith but has no deeds? Can such faith save them? Suppose a brother or a sister is without clothes and daily food. If one of you says to them, "Go in peace; keep warm and well fed," but does nothing about their physical needs, what good is it?
>
> JAMES 2:5, 8, 14-16

With the verses from James ringing in my ears, I told Junior to hang on a minute. Reluctant in my spirit but willing in my flesh, I walked from my front door to my bathroom and got him my fancy green razor. Once back at the door, I handed it over to him, and along with the razor I surrendered a bit of my immature entitlement. Having done my duty, I went back to my desk to continue writing lessons and letters.

I occasionally peeked out the window to my front-porch steps to see how his shaving was going. He didn't have water

or soap or shaving cream, all things I considered require-
ments for a proper shave. Curiosity got the best of me, and I
went outside to check on him.

"How's it going, Junior?" I asked.

"Oh, I'm fine, Ms. Lisa," he replied while wiping the razor
on his sweatshirt.

"Do you want some water or something?"

"Oh, yes ma'am, that would be very nice. Junior would
appreciate it." I had grown accustomed to and fond of the
way he commonly referred to himself in the third person.

"Here you go, Junior," I said as I returned with a cup
of water and sat it next to him on the porch steps, ready to
return inside.

"Do you know how to shave?" he followed up.

"Well, Junior, I guess so, but I've never shaved a person's
face." I responded slowly and nervously.

"Will you shave my face?" he replied, unfazed by my lack
of experience and obvious trepidation.

"Um. I guess so," was the best response I could muster as
I sat down next to him on my front-porch steps and began
to shave his face.

My nervousness wore off quickly because I could tell he
trusted me, and somehow, I sensed that I could trust him too.
I shaved his face carefully so as not to injure or harm him. I
shaved his face carefully because there was something about
those moments that felt truly sacred.

We had a great conversation while we sat on the steps. He
shared what it was like growing up as an African American in

Lake Charles, Louisiana, in the 1930s. He recounted stories of his mom and him sharecropping throughout Louisiana and Arkansas. I discovered that he lived a few blocks away in a boarding house. Curious how he made ends meet, I asked about his income and learned that he had been on disability for many years before now receiving regular Social Security checks. I learned that he could read, though not well. I learned that his mom had died in Fresno not far from where we were sitting. As I was finishing up his shave, I asked my neighbor-turning-friend, "Junior, when is your birthday?" His response came quickly and joyfully, "December the 25th."

"Really? December 25th?" I asked, surprised and excited.

"Yes, that's right. Junior's birthday is December 25th," he confirmed.

"Do you know who you share a birthday with, Junior?" I replied.

"Yes, I share a birthday with Jesus," he responded confidently.

There was a Jesus-ness about Junior that was undeniable. Perhaps it took the coincidence of a shared birthday to force to the surface of my consciousness the profound truth revealed in Jesus' words from Matthew 25:40: "Whatever you did for one of the least of these brothers and sisters of mine, you did for me." When I took time to care for Junior, an aged, materially poor man with a mental disability, it was as if I were taking care of Jesus. How that works out theologically, I may not fully understand. What I do know is that

Jesus has chosen to tether his identity to those who are poor and on the margins. When we encounter the least of these, we find Jesus, but oftentimes we must fix our eyes to see past his "distressing disguise."[1]

Junior and I remained friends for several more years. Despite my excellent shaving skills, he never asked me to shave his face again, though I would have in a heartbeat. Most times he asked for work, for food, or for money. Sometimes I met his needs, and other times I didn't. With each response, I tried to be faithful to Jesus. Some days when Junior came by, he didn't ask for anything. He simply wanted to visit and share friendship.

Junior wasn't a teacher just to me; he taught all the students and interns who came through the program. He never exposited the Scriptures. He never lectured about how to effectively love the poor. He showed up, and we learned. We fumbled forward together.

Late into his days on earth, Junior taught us how to love the sick and dying. He contracted cancer, and his body began to wither. We took him to doctors' appointments when he remembered to tell us about them. We cooked meals for him. We let him rest on our couches when he needed a cool, safe place to be comfortable in the Fresno summer heat. We prayed for him and sang the songs he asked us to sing when he was suffering and in pain. Eventually, when he became too frail to walk up the steps to his second-floor home, we carried him in our arms. We carried him because in so many ways he had carried us through the years. He had carried us out of our selfishness and entitlement. He had carried us out of a frenetic pace of busyness. He had carried us into greater generosity, deeper presence, and more meaningful relationship.

Who Is Worthy?

The breezy corridor of the small hospital in Nigeria where I worked was where I had my first encounter with Ruth.[2] I was immediately impressed by her strength and beauty. It wasn't so much her physical attributes that stood out to me, but more her sense of resolve and courage that shone through her eyes and smile as she ministered to the patients.

Ruth, like many "least of these," lives within intersections of vulnerability. She is a widow, she is poor, she is a single mom, and she lives positively with HIV. Her story, though marked with tragedy, also echoes with the beauty of redemption.

Ruth lived a relatively stable, middle-class life. She had a good education. She found love and was married. Together she and her husband had a son. Ruth was a faithful, good wife and mother. Years into marriage and motherhood, she began experiencing prolonged sicknesses that eventually led her to be tested for HIV. Her positive diagnosis was devastating not only because of its health consequences but also for its social ramifications. It revealed her husband's infidelity. Despite her own faithfulness, Ruth now carried a disease that he contracted from another lover and passed on to her.

Her husband's health declined more quickly than hers. His HIV deteriorated into AIDS and eventually took his life.

When this happened, Ruth's suffering increased exponentially. As was a fairly common custom, her in-laws blamed her for her husband's death and subsequently stripped her of everything. Her car, her home (including all her possessions), and most devastatingly, her son were all taken from her. She was left with nothing but anguish, the stigma of HIV, and a body wasting away with disease.

By God's grace, her story doesn't end with shame and destitution. A confluence of circumstances that included a Nigerian Christian doctor, a program implemented by then President George W. Bush, and a local hospital/clinic that restored hope through medical and social support groups provided Ruth with not only the medications she needed to recover but the affirmation of her dignity and value regardless of her disease status. The community surrounded her with hope and tangible assistance. She learned valuable job skills and after some time took on a pastoral role in her community. Her relationship with her son was also eventually reestablished.

The strength and beauty that welled up from her sense of dignity and purpose resulted from being seen by a God who is near to and identifies with the brokenhearted. Moreover, those who took seriously the words of Jesus in Matthew 25:36, "I was sick and you looked after me," made it possible for me to know Ruth and bear witness to the beautiful redemption story that played out in her life.

Even as I convey Ruth's story, I am aware of the risk of sharing it.

Though it poses no danger to her, it runs the risk of being

overlooked and squandered. Her story is centered in a place that is incredibly distant for most of us. Her sickness is one that perhaps still carries a stigma for some since it is primarily transmitted through sexual contact. A faraway place combined with a somewhat controversial sickness is a perfect recipe for disregard.

But, friend, disregard and distance aren't options for those of us who are members of one body (1 Corinthians 12:12). We are reminded by Paul in his letter to the Corinthian church, "God has put the body together, giving greater honor to the parts that lacked it, so that there should be no division in the body, but that its parts should have equal concern for each other. If one part suffers, every part suffers with it; if one part is honored, every part rejoices with it" (1 Corinthians 12:24-26). Ruth is a neighbor who cannot be disregarded. She is a part of the body of Christ, and her story is our story.

If we will have eyes to see Ruth as a neighbor, then surely we can see those in our own communities who, like Ruth, are among the least of these and deserving of God's care and concern. The intersections of vulnerability in Ruth's story of poverty, loss, and infirmity are intersections we come across daily in the lives of people who are near to us. We have Ruths in our midst. You have Ruths in your midst: in your church, in your office, on your block.

Who knows but that the Ruths in your life will not only serve as a vehicle for you to be God's love to them but also for your own life to be transformed? The truth is that we are renewed and liberated together, and our redemption is bound up with one another's through the work of Jesus' sacrifice and resurrection. We are bound together, and we need one another.

Will we have eyes to see and hearts courageous enough to respond? Can we hold space for those both proximate and distant? Will we be moved to action on behalf of those who have sicknesses that hold stigma and those who don't hold stigma? Rather than determining the "least of these" as worthy or unworthy based on our personal criteria, the question is *Will* we *be found worthy of the high calling we have received in Jesus to demonstrate God's compassionate care for the vulnerable?*

The Dusty Jericho Road

It was the middle of dry season when I met Pablo.[3] I still remember the dusty roads leading up to the compound where he had been staying as an asylum seeker just south of the US border in Ciudad Juárez, Mexico. Upon arriving, our group walked around the property that had once been a school. Small, bright-yellow cement buildings with green trim and green roofs were spaced out around a vast field of dirt and dust. Those small buildings once housed children who had come to school to learn. There was a playground of sorts in the center. It was bordered by semicircle tire remnants that had lost their vibrant pink, yellow, and blue paint colors. The tires were placed on their ends and secured firmly into the ground so that the children would know the bounds of the field and could enjoy the challenge of jumping from one tire top to the next. Two seesaws, one swing set, and two soccer goals made an otherwise giant dust patch a play place for the children who had journeyed with their families *al norte* (to the north).

After walking around the property, we were ushered into a dimly lit room with white-and-black-checkered tile floors and metal folding chairs arranged in a circle. Children's drawings hung around the room like clinging promises of hope. They were signs of both resistance to and defiance against even the darkest of despairs. Emily Dickinson wrote, "'Hope' is the thing with feathers - / That perches in the soul - / And sings the tune without the words - / and never stops - at all -."[4] The coloring pages of the migrant children had hope feathers, and they adorned the walls of that dimly lit room.

We were introduced to Pablo, a young man in his twenties. There was kindness in his face, though it was obvious that he had traveled a long, hard road.

Pablo chronicled his story through our translator. He was supporting a political candidate who was running against a long-time corrupt leader. One tragic day he witnessed the beating and attempted violation of a young girl by members of the opposing politician's staff. He intervened to save her. He immediately began to receive threats. His older brother, who joined him in supporting the new political candidate, suffered a brutal, near-death beating at the hands of supporters of the corrupt politician. Pablo began to also receive threats against his wife and children, and he knew he must leave in order to keep them safe. His wife was pregnant at the time. Amid her own grief at the tremendous loss she would experience, she posed a perfectly human and still agonizing question: "Why did you have to intervene when they were hurting that little girl? You didn't even know her." Pablo responded, "If I had a daughter, I would want someone to do for her what I did for that child. I would want someone to step in. I would want her to be protected."

Torn between the awful realities of endangering their lives with his presence or living without those he loved most dearly in this life, he did the unimaginable. Pablo said goodbye to his wife and two young sons. He made his way north with a letter from the political leader he supported that affirmed the endangerment of his life. This was his greatest proof of being a political asylee.

Upon arriving at the US southern border, Pablo requested asylum and was ordered to return to Mexico to await his immigration hearings. This immediate denial of admittance to an asylum seeker was due to a policy called Migrant Protection Protocols (MPPs) that required nearly all asylum seekers to remain in Mexico while awaiting their court dates. They were legally not allowed to work and faced extremely dangerous conditions at the border. The National Immigration Forum explains:

> A Medecins Sans Frontieres (MSF) report found that 75% of migrants returned to Mexico under MPP had been a victim of an attempted kidnapping, and

nearly 80% of migrants enrolled in MPP that were treated by an MSF mental health clinic at the border had been the victim of violence.[5]

As dusty and desolate as it was, being at this migrant shelter was a blessing for Pablo. While he experienced occasional minor violence at the hands of locals, he had the comfort of a roof over his head and the safety of four solid walls to sleep within. Many other migrants were in far more vulnerable situations, living in tents under bridges and along busy streets in Ciudad Juárez. Still, the days were long and difficult, waiting, wondering, hoping, and living in the liminal space of unbelonging. He didn't belong in Mexico, he no longer belonged in Guatemala, and he was wondering if he could belong in America.

Pablo had been in touch with his wife a few times during his months-long stay at the shelter. She missed him desperately and longed for his return. His court date was three weeks from the time of my team's visit. He concluded his story and pleaded for us to be praying for a positive outcome to his court hearing. Finally, he shared that his wife had given birth. To a daughter.

The journey from Central American countries to the US southern border is a modern-day Jericho Road. Often those who travel it are desperate and feel forced to choose between tremendously difficult circumstances. The promise of potential, with no guarantees of prosperity or security, merely the possibility of them, is sufficient reason for the thousands of migrants who journey north. I don't know the outcome of Pablo's case. It's almost certain he was denied asylum despite the endangerment to his life.

Imagine for a moment, however, if Pablo had made it through our borders either with or without authorization. What if he showed up in your community? Would you see him? How would you perceive him? What internal resistances surface for you as you imagine Pablo in your context?

God's preferential concern for the poor and the immigrant is clear in Scripture. We are to love them as we love ourselves (Leviticus 19:34). The pressing question is *What does love look like? How does it take action?* Love is nothing if it is merely sentimental. God did not love us sentimentally from a distance, with no action or consequence. He loved sacrificially in and through the person of Jesus.

Options abound for ways to demonstrate a faithful Christian response to the Pablos in our communities and at our borders. You can demonstrate hospitality and welcome by supporting organizations that work with migrant shelters just south of the border. Taking a learning trip to the border to visit these organizations would be an even more tangible and transformative experience.

In reality, very few of us are proximate to the border, and proximity matters to our discipleship and our witness. Faithfulness can look like volunteering to teach English or provide childcare for parents learning English after arriving in our country. Solidarity can take the form of helping those who need trustworthy lawyers find good legal counsel or connecting the newly arrived to resettlement and immigrant support agencies like World Relief, Lutheran Social Services, and Catholic Charities. Further actions could involve gaining a deeper understanding of the US immigration system and its need for comprehensive and fair reform, then taking steps to advocate for that type of reform. On a local level, helping ensure adequate ESL services are provided for immigrant children in school systems would be a representation of God's love and concern for these vulnerable neighbors.

We are God's hands and feet in this world. When we demonstrate biblical hospitality (*philoxenia*), literally love of strangers, we are told in Hebrews that we may be entertaining angels unaware (Hebrews 13:2). There are Pablos in our communities. There are Pablos still awaiting permission to make their way to our communities. As Christians, it is our duty and privilege to care for our immigrant and refugee neighbors. How will you see and respond to this beautiful responsibility and opportunity? When we consider the question *Who is my neighbor?*, do we see immigrants as our neighbors? Do we also see beyond our borders and recognize as our neighbors those who come in migrant caravans, those who live in tents under the bridges just on the other side of the Rio Grande?

God's eyes do not see the Rio Grande or any other border as the delineation between "neighbor" and "not neighbor." As people who have set our hearts on the ways of God and being fashioned increasingly in the likeness of Christ, we are invited to see with God's eyes and love our immigrant neighbors as ourselves. In this way, the power of God's love is demonstrated to those in need and we are transformed by our encounters with the stranger we invite in (Matthew 25:43).

Dismantling the Barriers

The "least of these" are all around us. What's more, they *are* us. When we engage in acts of compassion, we take steps toward centering the margins. Father Greg Boyle says it this way: "Compassion isn't just about feeling the pain of others; it's about bringing them in toward yourself. If we love what God loves, then, in compassion, margins get erased. 'Be compassionate as God is compassionate,' means the dismantling of barriers that exclude."[6]

Will we be those who dismantle the barriers of exclusion? Will we see the least of these as our neighbors and love them? Where will you begin? How can you meet and serve Jesus in even his most distressing disguises?

2

CREATED IN HIS IMAGE

David Hionides

WHAT ARE HUMANS?

Humanity has pondered this question for thousands of years. We are familiar with the famous words asked of God in Psalm 8:4—"What are human beings that you are mindful of them, mortals that you care for them?" (NRSVA). The question is a deeply reflective and piercing one. We want to understand who we are and our place in creation. As created creatures we look around with the psalmist and behold the heavens and earth. Mighty works of God that reflect his majesty fill the cosmos. What are we within this good creation?

Finding answers to the question remains a laborious task. We created an entire field of study to understand our humanity, and theological reflection on humanity offers much for us to ponder. One aspect that we study, and yet all too often still neglect to appreciate, focuses on what it means for us to be made in the image of God. This beautiful and majestic doctrine of Christian faith sheds light on the ancient self-reflection of Psalm 8. Its importance on how we live our daily lives, how we interact with others, and the motive it gives us for our sacrificial living flows from this doctrine as we better understand who we are as humans.

Scripture states that we are made in the image of God (Genesis 1:27). No other creation of God is said to be made in his image. It is a unique quality of humanity in the Creation narrative (Genesis 1:26). In light of this, Christians have long understood humans to be distinctly positioned as the pinnacle of all creation. Yet, as is often the case in Scripture, this doctrine remains simply stated but not defined for us. Theologians have long discussed what it means to be made in God's image.

Throughout history, various theories have been put forth relating to both the form and function of humans. Noting that the Creation narrative singles out humanity as being made in the divine image and likeness, Christians have sought to work out what this means by contemplating ways human beings resemble the triune God while remaining distinct from the rest of creation. From thinking along these lines arose the notion that "created in God's image" means we have the ability to reason. This notion led to some awful consequences. Humans seem to have differing capacities to reason. As a result, this interpretation all too often meant that those perceived as having less ability to reason were viewed as inferior, or even worse, not made in God's image.

Some people were viewed as created in the divine image to a great extent, others to a lesser extent, and some not at all and thus supposedly on par with animals. This interpretation then ushered in oppression and other mistreatment of marginalized populations, even including genocide and the destruction of our environment.[1] Such inhumane consequences have lessened the appetite for this interpretation. Additionally, continued research in the natural sciences (especially the thinking, learning, and even teaching capacity of creatures within the animal kingdom) further diminished this interpretation.

More recently, the dominant interpretation shifted to a "functional" perspective of creation in God's image. In this interpretation, humans function in a divinely appointed role. They serve as agents or representatives of God on earth. God gave them responsibility over creation. After creating humanity in his image and likeness, God explicitly tasks humans with ruling over the earth, entrusting them with stewardship of his good creation (Genesis 1:28). However, this textual connection found in Genesis 1 between the concept of rulership and creation in the divine image seems lacking in other related passages. Additionally, the problem of different capacities among humans' ability to rule well over creation have unfortunately moved some to again add discriminatory attitudes toward others, arguing that not all people are equally made in God's image and likeness.

Studies on the passage usually focus on these theories and interpretations, but rarely do they move on to understanding the ramifications of being made in the divine image. This leaves the wonder and magnitude of this basic Christian belief woefully ignored and unappreciated. Humans *are* made in the image of God, and this ought to impact how we view and treat each other. This Christian doctrine should lead us to a greater appreciation for all of humanity.

The Image and Likeness of God

Understanding what it means for us to be made in the image and likeness of God ought to be informed by what the image of God is. Thankfully, Scripture explicitly tells us what it is, or rather who it is—Jesus Christ. Colossians 1:15 states this truth for us clearly: The second person of the Trinity is the image of God. The invisible God became visible at the Incarnation.

That means we are made in the image of *Christ*. Whatever we believe or say about being made in God's image ought to be directly tied to the person of Jesus. It is his image and likeness in which we are made. This truth helps us avoid thinking that we *are* the image of God, or that the image of God is some abstract concept with little value or importance. It helps us understand the privilege that our creation entails.

The meaning of being created in the image of something is wholly dependent on the image itself. We are not simply made in the image of a common thing or even something majestic. Humanity is made in the image of perfection, in the image of perfect goodness, perfect power, perfect knowledge. We are made in the likeness of him whose glory and honor endures infinitely, whose goodness and majesty continues boundlessly.[2] We are created by God in this way; he elevated us toward his own perfection.

Knowing who the image of God is informs our comprehension of the meaning of this aspect of our creation. The image of God is Christ. The likeness that we were created in is that of Christ. The magnitude of this reality may be difficult to fully fathom. After all, as finite creatures we are trying to consider infinite perfection. Despite the difficulty of comprehending God's glory, recognizing Christ as the image of God reveals the important impact that being made in his likeness has on our daily lives.

A Familial Connection

While Scripture does not offer us a dictionary definition for what it means to be made in the image and likeness of God, the opening chapters of Genesis offer helpful connections for us. A few chapters following the Creation narrative, we once again read of someone being in the likeness and image of another. Genesis 5:3 informs readers that Eve and Adam's child Seth is born in the image and likeness of his father.

No matter what else one may understand about creation in the likeness and image of God, we see here that there is a familial connection. Christians know well the concept of being adopted into the family and household of God.[3] Yet here we are reading about a familial relation to God at the creation of humanity—and not limited to Christians. The implication for us is significant. Being human means having an intimate family connection to God. We are all his daughters and sons. God created people to be related to himself. By our very design we are more than simply a creation independent of its creator. We, as humans, exist as members of God's family, intentionally and specially related to him because he made us in his likeness.

The Whole Person

Christian belief sometimes swims upstream from the world's understanding. From the time of the Incarnation until now, human beings have been regularly perceived as little more than the various systems we're made of, a perception that reduces us to a mere hierarchy of elements. Common understandings of humans as Body-Soul, Mind-Body, or Heart-Mind-Body have all diminished the importance of our bodies. Some churches have even taught us that the "real me" is not our bodies, that our bodies are mere shells that hold our true selves. But the Scriptures reveal that while we have distinct parts, humans exist as unified beings, and our physical bodies are a vital piece of who we are.[4]

Rather than our humanity being encased *in* our bodies, it *includes* our bodies. When God made us in his image, he made us with the mud, the dirt, the earth, and added his breath (Genesis 2:7). God created us, in part, to be physical creatures. While we are more than just our bodies, we are not less than them. Creation in the likeness of God is not limited to our minds, our souls, or our hearts. Our full humanity, the entire package, our whole person was made in the divine likeness. This means our souls, spirits, minds, and bodies matter. Scripture repeatedly reflects this truth, calling our bodies the very temple of God and commanding us to honor God with our bodies (1 Corinthians 3:16-17; 6:19-20).

To be a human is to have a body. Understanding this fact helps explain why death is such a problem. We read in Scripture explicitly that death is our enemy. Death is the result of sin, a corruption of creation, and directly opposes our God, who describes himself as life (John 14:6). It results in the evisceration of our humanity, tearing asunder the intimate connection between body and soul. Thankfully our God is victorious over death; we will be given new physical bodies, and our humanity will be brought back to us at our resurrection.

Christ, who is the image of God, never modeled humanity apart from a physical form. Christ was born, lived, and breathed with a physical body. He was resurrected and now lives and breathes with a physical body. Christ became a human, he became flesh and blood, and dwelt among us (John 1:14). Following his death, he resurrected into flesh and blood. The disciples touched his physical body, such as when Thomas reached out and put his hand in Jesus' side (John 20:24-29). He felt the remnants of Christ's painful death; he touched the physical body of our resurrected

Lord. Christ ascended into heaven in bodily form, remains flesh and blood, and will return with his body. Since the Incarnation, the image of God eternally exists as a visible person with a physical body.

When we ponder what it means for us to be made in the image of God, we contemplate the whole of our person, both the material and the immaterial. If we neglect to include one part of our humanity in our understanding of being human, we fail to recognize the fullness of our privileged creation.

All of Humanity

In Western societies we often focus on the individual over the community. We focus on how something affects a person rather than how it affects a collective group. But when we think of being made in the image of God, it is important to understand that whatever this is, whatever it means, it is true for every single human. God neither created only Eve in his image nor only Adam. God created *all* humans in his image. No levels, or classes, or distinctions between humans exist when contemplating our creation in the divine likeness. Humans are diverse, yet they remain unified in their privileged creation as the sons and daughters of God. We are all made in the image and likeness of God.

It could even be argued that one aspect of this privileged creation is the diversity within unity that humanity holds. God is one, and God is three persons. There is diversity between the three divine persons, yet they are unified. In a way, humans mirror this. We come in different shapes and sizes, with different ways of thinking, different ways of understanding the world. We are distinct from each other, yet we are all unified as one. We are all humans.

Thinking about our creation in the divine image, we must recognize that it is a "we." God made us *all* in his image. We are all partakers in this divine production. We all have the family connection. No human was left out. We all share this no matter what choices we make in life, no matter what we say, think, or do, no matter what family we are born into, or which culture(s) informs us. We all are made in the image of God.

Let this truth sink in. There is no one, not a single human, not made in the image of God. This means that those we love, those we like, those who seem repugnant to us, those whom we ignore, minimize, or look down on—they are all made in the image of God, just as we are. All people, regardless of sex, ethnicity, nationality, mental or physical capacity, or any other distinction we can conceive, are made in God's image. We are unified in this truth regardless of any aspect of our diversity.

All too often we have abused our God-given diversity—that which we were created purposefully with—and have created separation and disharmony. Instead, we ought to understand, respect, and celebrate each other's diversity, seeking to unite and create a harmonious melody. This is, after all, the Christian vision seen in Revelation 7:9-10, of coming together in a united diversity as together we praise and worship our God.

Being made in the image and likeness of God unifies us

all. We all reflect our creator in our unified diversity. None are missing this divine distinction. As a corporate body, humanity shares in this special aspect of our creation. Regardless of the significance (or lack thereof) our cultures assign to us, all human beings share the privilege of being created in the image and likeness of God.

More than Equal

As Christians, we rightly believe in human equality. Yet the truth that we are made in the image of God raises the bar well above equality. Christian faith calls us to move beyond the common ethic of the world and lifts even higher the standards by which we ought to live. We are indeed all equal in worth and value. Regardless of anything in our lives—be it our finances, our ethnicity, our nationality, our politics, our education, our skin tone, our roles in life, or any other thing by which we divide and categorize ourselves—we are all absolutely, unequivocally, equally precious. We are all, in body and soul, members of God's family.

Thankfully, we recognize this truth in theory; but we know all too well that in practice humanity has struggled to live this out across time and place. As Christians, we also struggle to live this out despite affirming its truth. Yet even if we were to successfully live out our belief in humanity's equality, we would still fall short of our calling to live lives worthy of our God (Ephesians 4:1). The Christian worldview forces us to go beyond equality. It compels us to an even greater principle. We are all equal, but that is not all that we are. We are all made in the image of God.

Think of it this way: Equality does not necessitate a high value. It just means that all the things which are equal have the same value. All pennies are equal. They all have a value of one cent. Pennies are equal, but in our world of ever-increasing inflation, they do not have a high value. How often do you stop to pick up a single penny? If you saw one in a pile of mud, would you risk getting your clothes dirty to collect it? Probably not. But if you saw a one-hundred-dollar bill in the mud, you'd take that risk. That pennies are equal does not imply that they hold great value.

Like pennies, people hold equality. But our equality does not drive our value. By crafting us in his image, God created humans with inherently great value. It is one thing to destroy a penny and quite another thing to destroy a person. In Genesis 9:6, we see the gravity of shedding human blood. In that verse, God connects the punishment for shedding human blood with its value due to our creation in the divine likeness. Taking another person's life is an atrocious act because humans are made in the image of God. Human beings are valuable.

And not simply valuable like gold or silver. Human value is hard to comprehend fully. Remember: God condescended. He came down to earth for our salvation. While God elevates us toward himself through our creation, God lowered himself toward us by taking on human likeness (Philippians 2:7). Christ, the image of God, took on the likeness of humanity.

He more than lowered himself and lived among us: He suffered as we suffer; he endured temptation, thirst, and hunger; he experienced life as a human; he faced the problems of this world, living as a lowly carpenter. He weathered insults and violent torture, and he sustained immense pain and anguish on the cross to the point of giving up his life for us. God died to save us. Humans are worth dying for. That is a value we don't often grasp when we look around at others.

Do we see that same value in those we find difficult to love? Do we understand that the people all around us, cast aside by society, ignored, and oppressed, are people made in the image of God? That they are created with such value that God would come down to earth and die for them? Because that is exactly who they are.

There is no one on earth, past, present, or future, who has more or less value than any other person. We are all made in the image of God. All of us. No one is excluded. This is who we are, and how we were "fearfully and wonderfully made" (Psalm 139:14).

Living Out This Truth

Coming to grips with our creation in the image and likeness of God radically adjusts our thinking and our actions. We first recognize the privilege and honor we have as the pinnacle of creation. We see the value humanity holds. We understand that these truths are for all people, no matter what society tells us about each other. We are all partakers of this divine dignity and value. We understand that our entire being was created this way. This shift to our thinking then necessarily affects our actions. As we read in James 2:26, faith without actions is dead.

We no longer can look down on others as less than us; we must affirm the equality of all humans by the way we live our lives. But more than that, we must show every single person the value that God has created them with. We must treat human beings with more than dignity. Those who look different than us, those who think differently than us, those who are different than us we must respect, value, and dignify with the worthiness they were created with.

The divine commands that fill the pages of Scripture to help those who are downtrodden, those who suffer, and those who are oppressed are bolstered when we understand their creation in the image of God.[5] We ought not follow these divine demands only because they are mandates; rather, we obey because we recognize the value God gave all people—a value derived from he who is the image of God. Humanity holds immense value because of the infinite value of Christ. Recognizing this value God gave to the whole person, including the physical, reinforces the divine mandates to feed the poor, shelter the homeless, seek justice for the oppressed, and welcome the foreigner.[6] We must care for the whole person because we are commanded to do so in light of the first chapter of Genesis. Every command instructing us to treat each other with dignity and equal value is penned with the biblical knowledge that the whole person is created in the divine likeness.

Our reflection on what it means for us to be made in the image and likeness of God connects to the consistent message of Scripture to love one another as ourselves (Matthew 22:39). Family is meant to love family. It offers us a rationale for placing others above ourselves (Philippians 2:3-4). It helps us see the value God sees in us so that we may treat everyone in light of their God-given worth. It gives a basis for our sacrifices for others. In so many ways, our thinking on humanity's creation directly influences our interactions with others.

The Bible's beautiful and majestic teaching on being made in God's image and likeness conveys the Christian worldview that upholds the value of humanity. We learn to love each other more with the love God has showered on us. We join in God's (co)mission to save humanity because we recognize how valuable we all are, even the least of these.

3

A HISTORY OF COMPASSION

Ben Virgo

On the twenty-fourth of May 1738, a small, slight, hawk-nosed scholar walked north through London. He had attended Evensong at St Paul's Cathedral. Sunset wasn't due for another couple of hours, but the recently completed cathedral, the warm scents, and the evidence of the fleeting pleasures of the city—that sense of potential which had once thrilled him with a feeling of opportunity—now sat like a stale, cynical, dusty smoke.

In his early years he had learned to be suspicious of impulses that did not lead to serious application and endeavor, and he had kept himself in check with a diligence which might have been familiar to the weariest Pharisee.

The fifteenth child of an Anglican clergyman who would go down in history as a difficult man,[1] and of Susanna, who would go down in history as one of its most inspiring mothers, he had observed examples of Christian ministry throughout his life—examples which he considered hypocritical. Missing the mark. Not matching up to a great, integrated, and authentic purpose.

He therefore decided that the difference must be made, and that he would be the one to make it.

The man's name was John Wesley.

While at Oxford University, he had enforced a standard of righteousness on himself that inspired other young scholars around him. One did not have to look far in Britain in the 1730s to see evidence of the fall of man. On some streets in London, every second house was a gin house; the gin craze became such a concern in the nation that Parliament passed five Acts in an attempt to control consumption of a drink that was devastating a generation.[2]

Wesley saw that something must be done.

Recognizing that the teachings of Jesus focused on the inner life before any outer works might be done, young Wesley began by working on himself. Other young men at Oxford joined him in his diligent life of rigorous discipline, and in due course they (inevitably) were mocked by other students as "the Holy Club."[3]

When the opportunity came, Wesley resolved that he would apply what he had learned to a congregation. He would multiply what he had done in himself through a body of men and women. And where better to do this than in the New World? He went as a missionary to Georgia. However, he had a dreadful time in Savannah. His rigorous demands, instructions, and conditions not only discouraged and condemned his congregation, they also—most painfully—bore no fruit in his own life. He who had gone to America with the answer found himself with questions.

With increasing despair, he found that he was inconsistent, cold, and closer to what Jesus had described as a hypocrite than a disciple, let alone a minister. Wesley's congregation sensed that they neither truly understood what he was preaching, nor that he had any personal affection for them. He was preaching the law—the ministry, as Paul had called it, of condemnation (2 Corinthians 3:9). Its fruit was death. When Wesley left the congregation after two years, it was more to a collective sigh of relief than to farewell tears.

So, London, May 1738. Wesley walked from St Paul's, past print works and publishers, paper and delivery boys . . . past Christchurch Greyfriars, the burial ground of the old Puritan pastor, Richard Baxter. Ahead stood London's Wall—ancient and venerable. He walked through the Aldersgate, past St Botolph's-without-Aldersgate, where his father had been curate for a year, and, as Wesley would record in his journal:

In the evening I went, very unwillingly, to a society in Aldersgate Street, where one was reading Luther's preface to the Epistle to the Romans. About a quarter before nine, while he was describing the change which God works in the heart by faith in Christ, I felt my heart strangely warmed. I felt I did trust in Christ, Christ alone for salvation; and an assurance was given me that he had taken away *my* sins, even *mine*, and saved *me* from the law of sin and death.[4]

John Wesley understood that evening, understood at last: The gospel isn't instructions; it's an announcement. *It is finished* (John 19:30). He has done it—*Jesus* has done it! But did it work? Yes! He rose!

When he understood this, Wesley started to preach it.

He preached it about forty thousand times.

When he died in 1791 at the unusually old age of eighty-seven, John Wesley was considered *the best loved man in England*.[5]

At that time, in France, a revolution against the rich was beginning. In France, the poor had risen up in bitterness with murder. In Britain, the poor had been given hope through the gospel. In his multivolume *History of England in the Eighteenth Century*, the great historian W. E. H. Lecky proposed: "It is scarcely an exaggeration to say that the scene which took place at that humble meeting in Aldersgate Street forms an epoch in English history. The conviction which then flashed upon one of the most powerful and most active intellects in England is the true source of English Methodism."[6] Another secular historian, J. H. Plumb, states: "By 1760

Methodism was easily the most highly coordinated body of opinion in the country, the most fervent, the most dynamic. Had it been bent on revolution in Church or State nothing could have stopped it. But then Methodism was not a religion *of* the poor but *for* the poor."[7]

This extended narrative goes to the very heart of the issue of this book because it answers the question *What changes the world?* It is an acknowledged fact of history that Christianity has changed the world. Hospitals, universities, schools, stability in government—even models of integrity in trade and industry can be shown to have their roots in Christianity. Not to mention reformation, revivals, and countless initiatives in local contexts among the poor.

But What Do We Mean by *Christianity*?

The life of Wesley powerfully illustrates the point that what actually changed the world was *not* that in May 1738, he decided to try a bit harder. On that day in Aldersgate Street, Wesley learned that someone else had tried *perfectly*—someone had rejoiced in doing the will of his holy Father, and that it was he who came, not to give instructions but to take the blame for sinners.

He came in love. *He* came to do a work, and *he did it.*

It was the consequences of *that message* that changed history. Wesley *had* tried hard. It hadn't worked. It brought condemnation. What brought change was the message of the love of God, the work of grace in the gospel of Jesus Christ.

As we consider the marginalized, the homeless, and the

hungry, our responses are nearly always emotional, if not visceral. There is a temptation, which was known to Wesley, to leapfrog the message of the gospel and *cut to activity*. The New Testament warns us against this temptation. In this chapter I will seek, with the aid of a handful of illustrations from history, to show that the people who brought the change in which we now stand didn't even set out to change history. They just got their roots into Jesus Christ. And as they abided in him—well, what did he say would happen? They bore fruit (John 15:5).

Lord Shaftesbury

For centuries, if you wanted to heat your home in Britain, you would use an open fire in a fireplace. If you had a fireplace, you had a chimney. Chimneys would get dirty, even blocked. Therefore, there were chimney sweeps. A chimney sweep was allowed to have an apprentice—as young as eight years old. However, that age was never checked, and chimney sweeps would have apprentices as young as four.

A four-year-old boy could be pushed up a chimney with a width similar to the diameter of a frisbee. Boys were stuck in chimneys for hours. They were maimed, and some died. Many died of a particularly painful cancer.

One man, a Christian politician, fought against this horrid practice and beat it.

At the same time there were shameful institutions called mental asylums where people with mental illness would be locked up and, literally, chained to the walls. Their beds were covered in straw without bedsheets. Entering into the doorway of these places, visitors found themselves retching. Hygiene had been one of the first things overlooked by the masters of these underfunded institutions.

The same Christian politician fought and ended this.

If you had children at that time, you could get them an education—if you had money. If you were a poor family, single-parent family, or if a child was an orphan, there was no one to teach them to read and write. Some retired church ministers and the London City Mission set up what they called the Ragged School. They taught these boys for free.

The same Christian politician endorsed, publicized, and became the honorary president of the Ragged Schools.

Not only did over three hundred thousand boys get an education through the Ragged Schools, some going on to become mayors of their cities, but these programs shamed the government. Free education became seen as "a good thing."

That Christian politician died on October 1, 1885. Six days later there was a funeral service for him at Westminster Abbey. On that day, all of London mourned. Boys were seen holding signs that read "I was a stranger and ye took me in, naked and ye clothed me."[8]

The man's name was Anthony Ashley Cooper, but he is remembered by his title: the Earl of Shaftesbury. Shaftesbury would go on to be honored with the most famous memorial in London—the Shaftesbury Memorial Fountain, which stands at Piccadilly Circus, London's busiest intersection.

Shaftesbury left his mark on the world: Models of free

education and standards of care were established following his fight for them. The idea that a child would be pushed into a chimney against his will is now an abomination to us, yet it had been normal. But in his own life, Shaftesbury was ridiculed and mocked. He turned down the invitation to senior governmental office because he knew he would lose the independence that he could use to help the poor.

What was the blueprint for this? What was the motivation?

Shaftesbury has told us himself: He was not fighting for his rights, he gave up his rights, he would die in financial need. He was drawing from the fountain of our Lord himself.

Now a figure of history, Shaftesbury changed the world—but his roots ran into living streams where the humblest sinner is invited for grace, pardon, and life.

John Newton and William Wilberforce

One hundred years before Shaftesbury lived a man at the other end of the social ladder—a man considered not only by his contemporaries but *by himself* as a vile wretch. A man who had seen almost unimaginable cruelty. His name was John Newton. Newton's father had been a ship's captain, and young John was born in London at Wapping on the north bank of the River Thames. The sound of ships' bells, the sight of high ship masts, and, at high tide, the scent of the sea from the river hung around him like inevitability.

His mother had been a doting, hopeful presence but when she died in his early childhood and his father remarried, John found himself somewhat overlooked in the new family. In due course, unsurprisingly, he found himself part of a ship's company, traveling the ocean as a junior officer.

The cargo he carried was men's and women's souls.

John Newton's ship was a slave ship.

The vast number of people who were taken into slavery is, of course, staggering—eleven million seems a likely number;[9] but it was stories not of huge numbers but of *individuals* which would, for years to come, deeply affect Newton. He was once on a ship where down in the hold were scores, possibly hundreds, of people being taken from their families, homes, and land, never to return. They had nothing.

Except for one person. What she had was her baby. Haunted by this woman's story, Newton later shared it in writing:

> A mate of a ship, in a long-boat, purchased a young woman, with a fine child, of about a year old, in her arms. In the night, the child cried much, and disturbed his sleep. He rose up in great anger, and swore, that if the child did not cease making such a noise, he would presently silence it. The child continued to cry. At length he rose up a second time, tore the child from the mother, and threw it into the sea. . . . It was not so easy to pacify the woman: [but] she was too valuable to be thrown overboard.[10]

Story after story bled with pain and horror.

John Newton himself was hated by the other sailors: He

had a bitter heart which would seep and spill from a septic, cruel mouth. He was especially critical and undermining of higher-ranking officers, even those who were friendly to him. When one such senior officer had had enough of him, Newton thought it prudent to leave work onboard and take up a position on the African coast. However, the work he went into was in the business of slaving. His colleagues were, predictably, merciless—but Newton was shocked to find that their ruthlessness extended to him. When he became seriously ill, rather than helping him, they neglected and even despised him. He was sometime relieved by strangers, even by slaves, who secretly fed him from their own meager provisions.[11]

On the night of March 21, 1748, Newton was awakened by the terrifying sound of water pouring through his cabin. He jumped from his bunk and started to climb to the deck, but the captain called up to him: "Mr. Newton! Come down here—bring me your knife!" The man who *did* go up on deck was immediately washed overboard, never to be seen again.

Below decks, a dozen men were bailing water. Within minutes, the ship had become a wreck—a section had come out from its side, and water was pouring in. Sailors desperately patched and plugged the holes, and John Newton found the ship's pump.

As he stood, pumping through the storm, Newton did something out of character.

Although they had only had the best part of seven years

together, his mother had left an impression on him. She had taught him the catechism, she had prayed for him, she had taught him the hymns of Isaac Watts—and in that instance, holding onto that pump, John Newton, the bitter-hearted atheist, prayed: "Lord, have mercy!"

Immediately, what came into his head was the question *What mercy can there be for* me?

And yet, he survived.

The next day, he got a Bible. As he looked through its pages he found not religious techniques, not a philosophy, not a manual for behavior. He found a Savior who died for his enemies. The man who would later write:

Amazing grace, how sweet the sound,
That saved a wretch like me . . .[12]

put his faith in Jesus Christ.

He went on to train for ministry and quietly became one of the most influential pastors in history. William Carey. Henry Martyn. William Cowper. Each man's life was changed by John Newton. Many others were changed whose names have been forgotten by history, but not by a gracious Savior.

On December 2, 1785, a young member of Parliament, twenty-six years old, wrote a message to John Newton.

I have had ten thousand doubts within myself, whether or not I should discover myself to you; but every argument against doing it has its foundation in pride. I am sure you will hold yourself bound to let no one living know of this application, or of my visit, till I release you from the obligation.[13]

The young member of Parliament was William Wilberforce.

Wilberforce had recently made a profession of faith in Christ and had quickly concluded that this was the end of his political career. There was no way that a Christian was going to make it in Parliament. He had known great success already and had seen how success was dependent on all the impulses contrary to his new life of dependence on a God of grace.

What should he now do? Train for church ministry?

He turned to this man of grace and truth—this example of gospel ministry—John Newton. He went and poured out his heart to the old man, and Newton advised him to stay in Parliament.

The two men sat together—divided by thirty-four years, by the extreme ends of their social classes, and by countless experiences unique to each other but joined by the blood of a young Jewish carpenter in whom they both trusted.

Newton could counsel Wilberforce from the heart, and gently he advised Wilberforce to stay in Parliament. Wilberforce began to attend Newton's church, where he heard the old sailor pouring out his heart in his sermons as he preached grace, the gospel, and Christ. Newton was not known as a great preacher, but people stated that they came because they sensed they were loved.[14]

It was two years later that Wilberforce felt his heart

burdened: "God Almighty has set before me two great objects, the suppression of the slave trade and the reformation of manners."[15]

He would go on to fight the slave trade for forty-six years.

Minor successes, promised support, failure, allegiance from unlikely angles, illness, acute mental strain, contempt from the king, hatred from Horatio Nelson, swelling public support, suspicion and slander in the press and in Parliament . . . all gave way on July 26, 1833.

Now an old man, resting in a house in Westminster, unwell, Wilberforce was disturbed by a visitor at the door. By news.

"They're free."

Over eight hundred thousand slaves were free.[16] He had done it.

Three days later, Wilberforce died.

Olaudah Equiano

The horrors of the slave trade can now be read from the perspective of the former African slave, Olaudah Equiano, who was himself stolen into slavery as a child:

One day, when all our people were gone out to their works as usual, and only I and my dear sister were left to mind the house, two men and a woman got over our walls, and in a moment seized us both; and, without giving us time to cry out, or make resistance, they stopped our mouths, and ran off with us into the nearest wood. . . . At last we came into a road which I believed I knew. I had now some hopes of being delivered; for we had advanced but a little way before I discovered some people at a distance, on which I began to cry out for their assistance; but my cries had no other effect than to make them tie me faster, and stop my mouth, and then they put me into a large sack. They also stopped my sister's mouth, and tied her hands; and in this manner we proceeded till we were out of the sight of these people.[17]

At length Equiano found himself on a slave ship that would have been similar to the one on which John Newton was a sailor. From his own pen we read about the tremendous suffering he endured, while at the same time we find the astonishing testimony of his discovery of the same gospel of the free grace of God in Jesus Christ:

In the evening of the same day, as I was reading and meditating on the fourth chapter of the Acts, twelfth verse, under the solemn apprehensions of eternity, and reflecting on my past actions, I began to think I had lived a moral life, and that I had a proper ground to believe I had an interest in the divine favour . . . in this deep consternation the Lord was pleased to break in upon my soul with his bright beams of heavenly light; and in an instant, as it were, removing the veil, and letting light into a dark place, Isa[iah]. xxv. 7. I saw clearly, with the eye of faith, the crucified Saviour bleeding on the cross on Mount Calvary: the Scriptures became an unsealed book, I saw myself a condemned criminal under the law, which came with its full force to my conscience, and when "the commandment came sin revived, and I died." I saw the Lord Jesus Christ in his humiliation, loaded and bearing my reproach, sin, and shame. I then clearly perceived, that by the deed of the law no flesh living could be justified. . . . Oh! the amazing things of that hour can never be told—it was joy in the Holy Ghost![18]

Equiano had suffered barbaric cruelty, but his testimony is the same as that of every gospel believer: He found Christ, not as a victim but as a sinner. What melted Equiano was the mercy of God and his debt to free grace.

Equiano is likely the least known of all these examples of God's grace, which leads naturally to the tender and glorious issue that many who have worked from the principle of gospel compassion have accepted and embraced: There is no record in the Gospels of the Prince of Peace telling his disciples to prioritize the powerful and wealthy. When God lived on earth in human flesh, he spent time with a woman at a well with a chaotic life. With sinners. With people whom he referred to as sick, in need of a doctor (Matthew 9:12). People whose conversions would not necessarily make headlines.

Elizabeth Fry

A woman who exemplified this priority was Elizabeth Fry. Born into a family of bankers in 1780, she married Joseph Fry, a banker, in 1800. She is accessible to us through extensive diaries in which we see articulate, gracious, gospel-founded hope. In her time the Bloody Code was in force in Britain—a brutal system that took the number of crimes punishable by the death penalty to over two hundred.[19] Burglary, coinage offenses, and forgery could be capital crimes.[20]

Unsurprisingly, prison conditions at this time were appalling—Newgate Prison, which had a women's section, saw over thirty people die in a year, not from executions but simply from the conditions.[21]

Elizabeth Fry believed that what these women needed was not harsher punishments but the gospel of Jesus Christ. She agitated to be allowed to speak to the prisoners. Although she was discouraged from doing so, in 1813 she managed to make her way in using family connections. Authorities had expected Fry to collide with danger and friction inside the prison. Instead, she experienced cooperation and respect from the prisoners. She was not only the first person they had met in the prison who wanted to be there but she also treated each woman as a *person*.

Fry returned again and again. She held regular Bible studies with groups of respectful women prisoners. She witnessed corrupt practices and poor conditions and even slept in the prison to draw attention to what was going on. When the King of Prussia, Frederick William IV, came to England in

1842, he so respected Elizabeth Fry's work that he visited her in Newgate Prison.[22]

In 1835 Fry was invited to speak to Parliament, where she said:

> If anyone wants a confirmation of the truth of
> Christianity, let him go and read the Scriptures
> in prison to poor sinners; you there see how the
> Gospel is exactly adapted to the fallen condition of
> man. It has strongly confirmed my faith; and I feel
> it to be the bounden duty of the Government and
> the country that these truths shall be administered
> in the manner most likely to conduce to the real
> reformation of the prisoner.[23]

Prison reform was only one of the causes Fry would successfully prosecute.

◆　　◆　　◆

John Wesley, Lord Shaftesbury, John Newton, William Wilberforce, Olaudah Equiano, Elizabeth Fry.

These people had little in common, but their lives changed history. The world is different because they lived. In this short chapter we have looked at people who brought about free education, the end of the slave trade, humane treatment of those with mental illness, the end of child slavery, and prison reform. The fruits that came from their lives conspicuously speak of a gracious God—one who loves the fatherless and remembers the poor. What theorists had proposed, these people accomplished.

Why? What was their strategy? One does not have to look far to find that these extremely fruitful men and women were not conspicuously impressive strategists. What joins them all together?

Jesus Christ once gave a very simple equation: "Abide in me, and I in you. As the branch cannot bear fruit of itself, except it abide in the vine; no more can ye, except ye abide in me" (John 15:4, KJV).

Not one of the people we've considered set out to change the world. Many others have tried to change the world. They've tended to be forgotten quickly or to go down in history as its monsters. But *these* people simply got their roots into Jesus Christ. They enjoyed him. They tasted and saw that he is good. They searched for him in his Word. They treasured their Bibles because there they found their Lord.

Read their lives: They were faithful with the small things, they delighted in Christ. Read their journals. You will be surprised; they may sound like yours. *I should be so much further on than I am . . . I feel cold at heart, but trust his Word . . . I found some light in the text of the gospel . . .*[24]

Church history tells us one thing: *There is a hero*, and he is the one who came to save. He is the one who gave his life to take the blame that we deserve. He is the one who is vindicated by the Spirit, beloved of the Father, worshiped in eternity. He is Jesus Christ.

DO NOT WITHHOLD GOOD

Dennis R. Edwards

THE MAGNITUDE OF HUMAN OPPRESSION is overwhelming. I grew up and later ministered as a pastor in New York City as well as in Washington, DC, and Minneapolis. I currently work as a professor in Chicago. Living and working in large cities has made me aware of injustice and also provided opportunities for me to experience it. My wife, who is a licensed clinical social worker, also has a keen sense of how societal structures favor some people while complicating and marginalizing the lives of others. You may have had the opportunity to visit other countries as I have and know that multitudes of people throughout the world barely survive while a relatively small minority possess excess material goods—more than they could ever use.

People respond to injustice in different ways. On the one hand, there are cynics who blame oppressed people for their predicament, while on the other hand, there are activists who grow weary trying to alleviate suffering. And separate from the activists and the cynics are many who appear indifferent to human suffering or who may be too bewildered to consider solutions to social inequity. Cynicism, inaction, or lack of concern, however, should never be Christian responses to injustice. Those who claim to be followers of Jesus ought to be the most attuned to injustice while simultaneously passionate about participating in God's mission for the world.

Social justice describes our concern for God's creation in ways that reflect God's love. God deemed creation *very good* (Genesis 1:31), but sin marred God's work. Social justice entails human efforts motivated and animated by God's Spirit to restore God's original intentions for the cosmos.[1] The entire Bible communicates God's passion for justice: Justice was central to ancient Israel's practices and became a defining feature of the Christian movement. Justice is relevant to all aspects of God's creation, ranging from individual needs to communal concerns to environmental stewardship.

This chapter, however, focuses on the aspects of Scripture's call for social justice as it pertains to those on the margins of society. Various factors contribute to marginalization, such as economic systems that allow for some people to be impoverished—or even enslaved—while others flourish. Ethnic and racial bigotry marginalizes people, disadvantaging them economically, educationally, and socially, as well as in other ways that can make life barely tolerable for them. Ableism creates a world that values bodies that function in conventional ways while dismissing or complicating the lives of those with a variety of physical differences.

In the subsequent sections, I will demonstrate that the Scriptures urge—even require—God's people to dismantle unjust systems and also to do what is good for human flourishing. Christians are not immune to the competitive human tendency that approaches a Darwinian "survival of the fittest" perspective. Some people blame victims for their relatively powerless situation but credit themselves for possessing ingenuity, industry, or divine favor that privileges them with life's necessities—and many of its luxuries. Such people appear oblivious to the way power and prejudice conspire to construct social hierarchies that abuse some while advancing others.

According to the Gospels, it was in the home of a man named Simon that a woman entered and anointed Jesus with expensive lotion that had been contained in a costly alabaster box (Matthew 26:6-13; Mark 14:3-9). Critics considered the woman's act of devotion wasteful, claiming that the lotion could have been sold and the proceeds given to impoverished people. Jesus responds, "The poor you will always have with you" (Mark 14:7). Some Christians seem to take the words of Jesus as a concession rather than a challenge. For those Christians, concern for impoverished people is a *back-burner* issue since Jesus seemed to indicate the fruitlessness of the task of helping them since there will always be people at the bottom of society's hierarchy.

Yet, if we pay attention to the overall ministry of Jesus, as well as to Scripture more broadly, we see that the perpetual presence of the poor signals that there is always work for God's people to do that attempts to restore—or at least mirror—God's original intentions for the *very good* creation. What follows is an examination of a few passages in both the Old and New Testaments that call God's people to practice justice. I selected passages from various sections of the Bible that are not the usual, popular ones that many Bible readers in the United States turn to when discussing social justice. After consideration of these passages, I conclude this chapter with an invitation for Christians not to be satisfied with performing a few charitable acts but to honor God through the ongoing and deliberate pursuit of justice.

Social Justice in the Old Testament

The Christian Old Testament derives from the Tanakh, the Jewish Bible. This acronym designates the three major sections: Torah ("instruction"), Nevi'im ("prophets"), and Ketuvim ("writings"). This section explores a passage in each of the three main divisions of the Tanakh to illustrate that social justice is a thread woven throughout the Old Testament. The Torah example comes from Deuteronomy, while Ezekiel represents the Prophets, and a passage from Job is the Ketuvim's contribution.

Regarding the Torah, Bible professor Bruce V. Malchow asserts: "The Israelite law codes show a great deal of concern with the plight of the deprived. The laws attempt to rectify this problem by preventing mistreatment of the poor and by mandating improvement of their lot."[2] Malchow's point is especially evident in the fifth book of the Torah, Deuteronomy, where Moses admonishes Israel to give just treatment to the most vulnerable, namely the impoverished, the immigrant, the orphan, and the widow. For example, "He [God] defends the cause of the fatherless and the widow, and loves the foreigner residing among you, giving them food and clothing" (Deuteronomy 10:18). In Deuteronomy 15, Moses focuses on debt: "At the end of every seven years you must cancel debts" (15:1). Furthermore, Moses makes the stark assertion that "there need be no poor people among you, for in the land the LORD your God is giving you to possess as your inheritance, he will richly bless you" (Deuteronomy 15:4). Yet, as if to cover all bases, Moses goes on to add, "If anyone is poor among your fellow Israelites in any of the towns of the land the LORD your God is giving you, do not be hardhearted or tightfisted toward them. Rather, be openhanded and freely lend them whatever they need" (Deuteronomy 15:7-8). Instead of offering the poor condemnation, blaming them for their condition, Israel was to give them relief. Old Testament professor Leslie J. Hoppe declares, "Deuteronomy not only forbids exploitation of the people who find themselves outside of the economic mainstream, it also calls for the Israelites to take specific actions to prevent the precarious position of those on society's margins from degenerating."[3] Deuteronomy contains many examples of the Torah's demand for Israel to practice social justice.

The prophetic books are also full of admonitions for justice, and some might come readily to mind for Bible readers, such as Amos's cry that justice careen like a waterfall and righteousness flow like a never-ending river (Amos 5:24)—a favorite passage for Rev. Dr. Martin Luther King Jr. Those notions of justice and righteousness, however, appear frequently in the Old Testament. Ezekiel 18, for example, makes clear that justice and righteousness are not merely acts of personal piety or self-restraint on matters of individual morality but encompass what might be called social justice. To make a point about each person's culpability before God, Ezekiel illustrates this, saying, "Suppose there is a righteous man who does what is just and right" (Ezekiel 18:5). This hypothetical righteous person not only avoids idolatry, obeys Israel's purity codes, and refrains from personal acts of theft and oppression, but actively seeks to alleviate oppression by feeding the hungry and clothing the naked (Ezekiel 18:6-17). In our time, Christians can sometimes be heard defining their faithfulness, or even holiness, in terms of *avoiding* particular people and certain sins, but the prophets—like Ezekiel—view social justice as part of faithfulness to God. Bible professor Moshe Weinfeld pointed out that for Ezekiel, "The ideal of *performing justice and righteousness* is not confined to abstention from evil; it consists primarily in doing good: giving bread to the hungry and clothing to the naked (Ezek. 18:7, 16)."[4] There are, of course, myriad other passages in the Prophets that make the same point as Ezekiel that faithfulness to God means caring for the most vulnerable.

Job provides an example from the Ketuvim where the protagonist's defense, in view of his inexplicable—at least to him—suffering, includes the poetically evocative image of being outfitted with justice and righteousness: "I put on righteousness as my clothing; justice was my robe and my turban" (Job 29:14). As with Deuteronomy and Ezekiel, Job describes justice and righteousness in terms of advocacy for the marginalized:

> I was eyes to the blind
>   and feet to the lame.
> I was a father to the needy;
>   I took up the case of the stranger.
> I broke the fangs of the wicked
>   and snatched the victims from their teeth.

JOB 29:15-17

Weinfeld suggests that what one observes in Job can be found throughout the Wisdom Literature.[5] The opening verse of the book of Job describes him as blameless, upright, fearing God, and avoiding evil (Job 1:1), yet Job's monologues help communicate that blameless and upright behavior includes helping to alleviate the suffering of impoverished and otherwise marginalized people.

The Tanakh, Israel's Scriptures, point out that God's people, who know the horrors of slavery, must not oppress foreigners, widows, or orphans (Exodus 22:21-22). Not only should God's people avoid oppressing those groups, but they must also provide for them because God defends and loves such people (Deuteronomy 10:18). A defining characteristic of God's people is that they—following God's own example—love, defend, and provide for the marginalized people within society.

Social Justice in the New Testament

As with the Old Testament, instructions to practice justice are ubiquitous throughout the New Testament, yet our analysis must be dense—possessing great weight while contained within a small volume. Three passages are presented here also, selected from different parts of the New Testament. Although the original audiences faced varied concerns, they had to learn that Jesus' teachings require justice for marginalized people. The three passages consist of one from the Gospels (Matthew 23:23), some verses from a Pauline epistle (Romans 12:13, 20), and finally a section from a general (or catholic) epistle (James 2:14-17). While these passages are contained in different sections of the New Testament, they each echo themes of justice, righteousness, and mercy found in the Old Testament.

Matthew 23 contains a series of seven prophetic indictments that Jesus makes against some Jewish leaders, each commencing with "woe to you" (verses 13, 15, 16, 23, 25,

27, 29). At the fourth indictment, Jesus denounces failure on the part of some Jewish leaders to practice justice. He says, "Woe to you, teachers of the law and Pharisees, you hypocrites! You give a tenth of your spices—mint, dill and cumin. But you have neglected the more important matters of the law—justice, mercy and faithfulness. You should have practiced the latter, without neglecting the former" (Matthew 23:23). Jesus does not disregard or abolish the Old Testament legal requirement to contribute a tithe from a family's produce (Leviticus 27:30), but he assigns greater importance to justice, mercy, and faithfulness. Those latter three virtues continue from Old Testament notions.[6] In fact, the trio of virtues mirrors what the prophet Micah admonishes:

> He has shown you, O mortal, what is good.
>   And what does the LORD require of you?
> To act justly and to love mercy
>   and to walk humbly with your God.
> MICAH 6:8

There is an obvious parallel with justice and mercy while Jesus says "faithfulness" rather than Micah's "walk humbly with your God."[7] But one can see that walking with God is tantamount to faithfulness. The more important matters are conspicuous and directly benefit others to a greater degree than contributing a tenth of one's herbs.

Romans 12 offers a series of practical instructions for the Christians in Rome, elucidating the implications of being "living sacrifices" who do not conform to the world's way of doing things but whose actions are transformed through the adoption of a new way of thinking (verses 1-2). In verse 13, Paul urges extending hospitality, which includes sharing resources with those who need practical assistance. The apostle's instructions accompany behaviors we readily accept as *spiritual*, such as loving, being zealous in Christian service, and being joyful, patient, and prayerful. Yet, right alongside such obvious devotional behavior is attending to the needs of those facing the daily pressures associated with poverty. Paul urges partnership or sharing (using the Greek verb *koinōneō*) with fellow believers who are struggling. With Paul's focus being on fellow believers, one might be tempted to assume that the apostle restricts acts of justice to those within the church community. However, a few verses later, Paul quotes Proverbs 25:21-22 when he addresses how to deal with those who might be hostile to the Christians in Rome:

> "If your enemy is hungry, feed him;
>   if he is thirsty, give him something to drink.
> In doing this, you will heap burning coals on his head."
>
> ROMANS 12:20

In Paul's admonition, not even enemies deserve to suffer injustice. The "burning coals" are symbolic, perhaps indicating the shame enemies might feel or the judgment they might encounter for bringing harm to God's people.[8] While the coals are symbolic, the food and drink are metonyms—merely representative of what a struggling person might need. Kindness, in the form of justice, is part of how to address antagonists—not with revenge (verse 19) or even indifference, but with concrete acts of mercy. The instructions in Romans 12 echo the words of Jesus, especially in Matthew 5, part of the Sermon on the Mount, and the overall tenor of the verses reminds Bible readers of the Lord Jesus Christ's own way of maneuvering through the world.

James 2:14-17 describes the absurdity of seeing a person in obvious physical need, proceeding to wish that person well, but not doing anything to address the need. Such ludicrous behavior indicates the vacuous nature of confessing correct doctrines without performing proper practices. Christian discipleship can often be more about "head" than "hands," which is to say that we might catechize people to recite information about God and Scripture but not instruct them to perform just behavior. When some Christians do address proper behavior for new converts, they tend to focus on a narrow arena, such as sexual activity, sobriety, honesty, and perhaps even basic benevolence such as giving money to the church, but the broader concepts of justice and mercy often get treated as some form of extra credit, if they are mentioned at all.

James refers to *adelphos hē adelpha* ("a brother or sister") who lacks sufficient food and clothing. Some Christians take "brother or sister" to indicate that social concern is to be restricted to those within the Christian community, as with Romans 12:13 (discussed above). For the sake of the argument, even if James intends such restriction, plenty of Christians withhold financial and other support for fellow Christians until those individuals meet certain criteria that demonstrates that they are somehow worthy of assistance. Indeed, when my wife and I were young parents striving to survive in expensive Brooklyn, New York, we learned that a member of the predominately white church we happened to attend had an apartment to rent at a reasonable price. We inquired only to have him tell us "My neighbors wouldn't want a Black family on the block." Despite the fact that my wife and I participated in the same congregation as that man and presumably shared a common faith in Jesus with him, we could not rent his apartment because of our race. James, rather than restricting the range of Christian love by mentioning "brother or sister," may simply be illustrating with a simple and likely example that faith without action is oxymoronic. A few verses earlier (verses 2-13), James dealt with the injustice of favoritism granted to a wealthy visitor to the church assembly over an impoverished guest. James addresses situations with strangers and with known Christian siblings and in each case makes the point that faith without action is dead.

Even though we explored only three passages, the New Testament consistently instructs Jesus followers to provide practical assistance—food, water, clothing, money—for those who lack, not in a *quid pro quo* fashion, expecting something in return, but because love for fellow human beings is a mark of faithfulness.

Love Does Not Tolerate Injustice

Christian discipleship needs to emphasize social justice. Seasoned Christians must teach newer converts the way of Jesus (Matthew 28:20), which entails modeling and communicating the importance of love for all of God's creation. Love seeks what is best for others—especially for those on the bottom of society's hierarchy, far away from the best that life might offer. Those beaten down by the vicissitudes of life, who suffer discrimination and alienation, require that the wrongs they face get righted. People are marginalized because of their ethnicity, race, gender, physical condition, low income, lack of formal education, and other factors, but love—which stimulates justice—strives to alleviate suffering for all of God's creation. Justice motivates those among God's people who have relatively plenty to share their lives with those who lack resources. Yet, people motivated by justice not only share their resources; they also work to dismantle the structures that cause their neighbor's pain. Christian discipleship must teach that love does not tolerate injustice. Confronting injustice is not an elective course in the curriculum of discipleship but is indeed required for successful matriculation into God's program for spiritual maturity.[9] The so-called great commandment—to love God and love neighbors (Mark 12:30-31)—means engaging in social justice.

The previous sampling of verses from a cross section of the Bible demonstrates that true devotion to God entails concern for those struggling in our world, whether they are members of our religious community or not. Such concern is part of what social justice entails. From our reading of Scripture, we note that society's alienated are not demonized, belittled, or shamed by God or God's people. Rather, those in dire need are to be offered what is necessary for life. Further examination of Scripture would point out that not only are God's people to perform charitable and benevolent acts for those in need, but upright people work to dismantle unjust systems. Indeed, Israel's prophets typically addressed their oracles to the kings and priests so that with proper leadership ancient Israel's entire way of life would line up with Torah values. For example, Isaiah 58, which gets read during the Jewish service of Yom Kippur, includes these words:

"Is not this the kind of fasting I have chosen:
to loose the chains of injustice
    and untie the cords of the yoke,
to set the oppressed free
    and break every yoke?
Is it not to share your food with the hungry
    and to provide the poor wanderer with shelter—
when you see the naked, to clothe them,
    and not to turn away from your own flesh and
    blood?"

ISAIAH 58:6-7

Penitent Jewish people in contemporary times remind themselves at least annually of what was true centuries ago: Devotion to God is not confined to religious rituals but is measured in how God's people treat vulnerable people. As the *Jewish Study Bible* notes regarding Isaiah 58, "Real humility toward God would engender a desire for justice toward the weak, compassion toward the downtrodden, and charity toward the poor."[10] The New Testament echoes the prophetic concerns of the Old Testament, as illustrated in James 1:27: "Religion that God our Father accepts as pure and faultless is this: to look after orphans and widows in their distress and to keep oneself from being polluted by the world." Discipleship in the way of Jesus emphasizes that how we treat others, especially those whom society has alienated and humiliated, is an indication of our faith in God. If we claim to have faith, then we strive for justice.

On a practical level, Christians ought to strategize continually to discover the best ways to practice social justice, but in the meantime we do whatever we can to help others. We need never withhold good even as we imagine increasingly better ways to address injustice. To paraphrase James 2:17, faith that doesn't put forth effort to alleviate injustice is a lifeless corpse.

THE COMPREHENSIVE GOSPEL

Brandon Washington

Social justice is not, moreover, simply an appendage to the evangelistic message; it is an intrinsic part of the whole, without which the preaching of the gospel itself is truncated. Theology devoid of social justice is a deforming weakness of much present-day evangelical witness.

CARL F. H. HENRY

I REMEMBER THE PRECISE MOMENT I embraced the gospel. It was during a small midweek Bible study on March 12, 1997. I was not there out of Christian devotion. After I'd disavowed the teachings of a segregationist Islamic cult, a friend invited me to church. My attendance was little more than an act of curiosity. The pastor was teaching a series on the apostle Paul's letter to the Ephesians, and we'd arrived at the first ten verses of the second chapter. After attending for a few months, the pastor had garnered my confidence. He was a trustworthy teacher, but on this particular Wednesday, for me at least, he was exceptionally coherent, and that provoked questions.

I waited for everyone to leave before offering my queries. I did so, in part, out of embarrassment; my questions could appear elementary to the others. I was also concerned about how long it would take to subdue my doubts; I didn't want to monopolize the group's time. After everyone left, the pastor and I sat in a vacuous sanctuary. He spent two hours rehearsing Ephesians 2 and supplementing it with additional Pauline texts. Before leaving that evening, I confessed Jesus as Lord, and the conviction persists to this day.

In retrospect, I am sure of two things. First, though I'd heard sermons, I never heard the gospel before March 12, 1997. To be clear, I am not asserting that I'd heard it without understanding it; I maintain that I'd never heard a careful and uncluttered account of the gospel. Never! I knew Jesus died, but I always understood it as martyrdom, not sacrifice. That midweek experience is the reason I now value a clear articulation of the gospel. If the message is garbled or plagued by haughty Christianese, then we are scandalously hiding it in plain sight (Romans 10:14). Second, my present-day understanding of God's role in Christian conversion spotlights the Holy Spirit as the star actor. The Spirit empowered my pastor and illumined his commendable presentation (John 14:26). The Spirit also softened my heart, freeing me to hear the appeal (1 Corinthians 12:3). The wooing of God made divine grace compelling and, dare I say it, irresistible.

All that to say that I take no credit for my conversion, but I readily recognize it as the most vital moment of my life. The gospel is, by far, the most important idea I've ever experienced. So imagine my dismay when I realized that I had, for years, truncated the message.

While I do not believe I was preaching a "different" or "accursed" gospel (Galatians 1:6-10, ESV), I confess that I espoused a partial account—one that looked forward to eternal deliverance with little regard for our temporal lives. A truncated gospel can be temporally damaging; it allows for ethical complacency. It adulterates biblical justice in a world that desperately needs the gospel's *shalom*—peace and wholeness.[1]

The Gospel Brings Wholeness to Brokenness

The evening of my conversion, my pastor taught me that the bond between humanity and God was grossly broken because of the Fall in Genesis 3. Blessedly, the gospel is the message of God's intervention—his bold plan to "bring wholeness to brokenness," as my pastor explained. God did not deploy weaponry or entrust the repair to fallen humanity. Instead, the second member of the Trinity, the *Logos*, the eternal Son, became the Incarnate One (John 1:14); God became human and reunited humanity to God via the monumental sacrifice. Christ is the hub; Paul's message in Ephesians 2 hinges on Jesus' intervention. But, in my estimation, this understanding of the gospel is woefully remiss because it overlooks an essential aspect of Christ's work.

A Partial Gospel

Our popular reading of Ephesians 2 is only a partial recognition of the gospel. We use Ephesians 2 to teach the doctrine of justification or eternal salvation—though even that language may be uncareful. The first half of the chapter has fallen prey to American evangelicalism's proud legacy as a "revivalist" tradition.[2] We've relegated the gospel to an escape plan.[3] Imagine an irreparably damaged ship sinking with thousands of potential victims aboard. Saving the ship is implausible, so the default plan is to marshal as many passengers as possible to lifeboats before the vessel disappears beneath the water's surface. Our emphasis on revivalism treats the gospel as tantamount to a lifeboat. For some time now, our message has been, essentially, "The world is beyond repair, and God will one day destroy it. Those who refuse to disassociate with the world by accepting Christ as Redeemer will eventually go down with the ship. But those who accept his invitation will spend eternity with him, experiencing bliss in a heavenly abode; we need only endure until he returns."

I cannot count the many occasions I've heard this revivalist message, or some form of it, blaring through speakers in a football stadium or arena, or from a well-intended preacher fulfilling pulpit duties. Even if we set aside its poor eschatology, the revivalist message always provokes questions. What if God intends to redeem the ship? What if we, empowered by the Spirit and armed with a comprehensive gospel, are how he tends to the world? I maintain that truncation of the message is, to some degree, provoked by our decision to stop at Ephesians 2:10. Verses 11-22 are essential to appreciating the comprehensive message, but these verses are inconvenient; for some, they are even scandalous. Paul's gospel insights do not stop at "getting people saved." He provided temporal implications of Christ's sacrificial work. Moreover, the temporal implications are *not* incidental; they are as fundamental to the gospel as eternal salvation. To ignore them is a disservice to Christ's whole work.

Ephesians 2:1-10

I fear casual readers may assume my critique is dismissive of Ephesians 2:1-10. On the contrary, the passage is foundational. Paul sets up the intervention of Christ by unveiling a clear and present need. From conception, humans are "dead in [our] transgressions and sins" (Ephesians 2:1). Spiritual death is universal because it is intrinsic to humanity. We participated in, and are therefore guilty of, the cosmic treason committed by Adam, our human representative, in the Garden (Genesis 3). We are *not* born merely infirm, weak, or wayward; these terms fall short of Paul's grave imagery. He carefully identifies the pre-Christ human condition as hostile toward God: "We were God's enemies" (Romans 5:10). A genuine desire for God is foreign to us. Instead, in our unredeemed state, we walk according to the dictates of a false lord, one whom Paul calls "the ruler of the kingdom of the air" (Ephesians 2:2). The obedience to an unworthy master occurs with our willing complicity, so "we were by nature deserving of [God's] wrath" (Ephesians 2:3). The verdict is inevitable; God is just, so our eternal condemnation is obligatory.

In Ephesians 2, Paul follows the template of an enthralling message; it's a multi-act story that unfolds toward a resolution. The first act of a good narrative introduces and spotlights a problem. Paul has presented a human condition that, if read honestly, consigns us to hopelessness—separated from God and woefully incapable of returning to his good graces. The spiritually dead are incapable of doing the work of the living. That is the problem. However, the bad news is the setup for good news. In verse 4, Paul turns the tension on its head with a pivotal word—*but*. For the rest of our lives, it is a term that should leap from every biblical text, especially when God is the subject.

Conjunction . . . What's Your Function?

As children, my brother and I woke early on Saturday mornings for our weekly cartoon tradition. We would plop in front of the television with bowls of cereal, mesmerized by animated entertainment we were deprived of during the week because of school and homework. Between the cartoons was a series of three-minute musical clips called *Schoolhouse Rock!* We thought they were entertaining and even catchy jingles, but they were also furtively educational. A decade later, when I was a freshman in college, I passed a Government midterm exam because I wrote, verbatim, the *Schoolhouse Rock!* jingle that explains how a bill becomes a law.[4] The professor was impressed by the answer; she noticed its meter, and that it rhymed. *Schoolhouse Rock!* was an asset to Generation X. If you are familiar with it, you know that the most excellent jingle they ever produced was "Conjunction Junction."[5] The image of the animated train conductor connecting train cars comes to mind every time I read Ephesians 2. He introduced us to English conjunctions and the utility of the word *but*. It can emphasize what comes after it as it deemphasizes what came before it. The bad news of verses 1-3 is turned on its head because verse 4 begins with "but."

Verse 4 is the reset button; it brings everything back to zero. So the contrast between verses 1-3 and verses 4-10 is stark. Before verse 4, we are "dead in [our] transgressions and sins"; after verse 4, we are "alive with Christ." Before verse 4, we followed the "ruler of the kingdom of the air"; after verse 4, we are "raised . . . up with Christ and seated . . . with him in the heavenly realms." Before verse 4, "we were by nature deserving of wrath"; after verse 4, we are "by grace . . . saved . . . through faith." For those who believe, eternal condemnation is divinely defeated by eternal adoption. The change results from the intervention of God, described by Paul in verse 4. Christ's sacrificial death is the means to our renewed relationship with God; he died in our place—bearing the penalty of our sin (Romans 5:8; 6:23)! It is a message worthy of unbridled celebration. But it is not the entirety of the message.

The Gospel's Other Domain

Among orthodox Christians, there is little conflict regarding the implications of the Cross on the reunion between God and humanity. In no uncertain terms, Paul presents the effectual work of Christ in verses 4-10. Our eternal condition is settled if we embrace his sacrifice "by grace

. . . through faith" (Ephesians 2:8). But Paul was not done. The latter half of Ephesians 2 is not a change of subject; Paul is expounding. He is addressing an additional domain of the gospel. Verses 11-22 follow the same format as verses 1-10. Paul presents a desperate condition—namely, a rift within humanity.[6] The ethnic divide between Jews and Gentiles was as brazen as the broken bond between humanity and God. In verses 11 and 12, Paul underlines nationalistic, theological, and sociological barriers—idols that contribute to a yawning chasm between various sects of human beings.

In verse 13, Paul rehearses the inversion that occurred in verse 4, and he uses the same conjunction, *but*. Just as God intervened in verse 4, graciously confronting the brokenness between God and humanity, he intervened in verse 13, graciously confronting the rift within humanity.[7] As a matter of fact, verses 4 and 13 refer to the same divine act! It was the Cross that reconciled humanity to God, and it is the Cross that *conciles* humanity; the gospel has vertical *and* horizontal implications.[8] Historically, we have emphasized the former to the exclusion of the latter. It is not necessarily a heretical view of the gospel; it is, however, a truncation that temporally diminishes the gospel.

According to Paul, one gospel unites us to God *and* one another. Preaching the former and ignoring the latter makes us purveyors of a partial message. The Savior's death, burial, resurrection, and ascension affords us the fruits of an eternal destination; it also affords Kingdom citizenship and ethics that, when honored, provide temporal wholeness. To this point, Paul reminds us that Christ is "our peace, who has made the two groups [Jews and Gentiles] one and has destroyed the barrier, the dividing wall of hostility" (Ephesians 2:14). In his "flesh," Christ brought unity, "[creating] in himself one new humanity out of the two" (verse 15). He accomplished this by shedding his precious blood on the Cross (verses 13, 16). The Cross is more than a lifeboat; it is life itself—both temporally and eternally. In sum, Paul asserts that our reunion at the feet of Christ prompts an inevitable union among Kingdom "citizens," a "household" that puts the King's character and values on display (verse 19).

The High Price of Our Union

You can always tell how much someone values something by noting how much they paid for it. My wife has observed where my values lie, and she cites a financial ledger as Exhibit A. Blissfully, I drive a thirteen-year-old car. I have a few shirts and even fewer pairs of jeans. I am unwilling to spend excessively on such things; it is a practical value that I proudly cite as evidence of my stewardship. But my wife, knowing me all too well, is quick to spotlight my library. She has chimed, "Brandon, you don't buy cars and clothes because you do not value such things. You do, however, have a room with thousands of books in it. It is what you care about, so it is where you spend money." She has biblical backup for her charge: "Where your treasure is, there your heart will be also" (Matthew 6:21). The truism has merit.

With that in mind, consider this: When it was time to pay the price to restore the relationship between God and humanity, the Father offered his Son, "with [whom he is] well pleased" (Matthew 3:17) as a sacrifice. We can all agree that so great an offering is worthy of our wholehearted surrender. It is evidence of God's high affection for those who bear his image. He did not need us, yet he sacrificed the highest price to have us. It speaks to his divine affection for beings made in his image (Genesis 1:27; John 3:16). Now consider that the same sacrifice was paid for us to have one another, and it empowers us to be animated icons who put his Kingdom's culture on display (Matthew 6:10). If the apostle Paul is correct, and he is, the same Cross that eternally saves us also commissions and equips us to seek out human conciliation and be activistic toward humanity's wholeness in the world. It meant so much to God that he paid the highest price. So, armed with the gospel, we advocate for the Kingdom—graciously confronting all that is unlike the Kingdom's culture. Otherwise, we are advocates of a reductionistic and somewhat impotent message.

Gospelizing the World

God commissioned the church with the task of gospelizing the world (Matthew 28:16-20; Acts 1:8; 1 Peter 1:25). It is an imperative that requires a comprehensive gospel. Unfortunately, we've reduced the message to a means of eternal escape. Our mission, it seems, is little more than punching heaven-bound tickets and telling converts to endure a fallen world until Christ returns.[9] For over a decade, I've grappled with our error and the damage it causes. As a Black man, I am attentive to and wounded by American evangelicalism's history of gospel reductionism. I align with the evangelical camp, but I've observed a history of theological and ethical abdications that resulted from an unholy abridgment of the Cross.

For instance, the Great Awakening is lauded as a season of Christian confessions culminating in heavenly destinations. Conversions and the proliferation of Christian culture are cited as evidence of the Great Awakening's worth. But I'd be remiss if I did not spotlight the willingness to sit idly by as human beings, image bearers, endured an ethnic caste system, slavery, and inhumane subordination during America's era of abundant Christian conversions. What's worse, the church was willingly indifferent and even complicit in the inhumanity. It is an affront to our comprehensive message.

George Whitefield was the most well-known preacher of the Great Awakening, one of the most famous people in the world. His notoriety was the product of his competence as a communicator. He had a reputation for uncompromising oratory to the glory of Christ. Attendance was impressive during his open-air revivals, and conversions occurred in droves. Undoubtedly, his success derived from his capacity to preach *a* gospel message. He convincingly introduced the sinful hopelessness of humanity, and then he turned it on its head by introducing the compelling intervention of Christ. Whitefield is lauded as a quintessential gospelizer; he fulfilled the great commission and published Jesus' eternal impact on the world. I concede that his admirers can justly argue that he played a formative role in church history.[10]

Here's the rub: Regarding ethnic wholeness and justice in the world, Whitefield's gospel message willfully excluded the accomplishments of Christ. He was not merely indifferent toward slavery; he was an active, unashamed enslaver![11] He consciously resisted abolitionism and advocated for the legalization of slavery in Georgia. He flew the banners of gospel preacher *and* enslaver. How can both be true? Historian Thomas Kidd writes, "To Whitefield, benevolence to slaves primarily entailed introducing them to the gospel."[12] Whitefield conceded the humanity of enslaved Africans and the need to preach a message that secured their eternal destiny. But the message stopped conveniently short of their earthly wholeness. An evangelical stalwart preached a truncated gospel that valued eternity while it prolonged and increased temporal brokenness. His actions were inevitable fruits of a partial message! He preached Ephesians 2, but as it relates to slavery, verses 11-22 were excised from his understanding of the gospel.

Whitefield was not an outlier. Jonathan Edwards, another stalwart of the Great Awakening, was an enslaver; he preached at least one sermon defending it.[13] American segregation was upheld by artificial racial differences and nationalistic values that are reminiscent of the rift in Ephesians 2:11-12.[14] The Civil Rights movement was critically scrutinized by clergy members who thought the movement's leaders were not sympathetic to the South's traditions and sensitivities.[15] And even the twenty-first century finds us debating which aspect of our past should be obscured to preserve the misleading narrative of an unmarred Christian history. While such abhorrent behavior is expected from a fallen world, for Christians it is a violation of the message afforded us by the Cross. The church's peculiar participation in earthly brokenness results from espousing a truncated gospel. We have embraced a message that is so heavenly minded that we are, in too many regards, of little earthly good.

Repent, and Return to Our First Love

The sacrifice of Christ for our eternal salvation has been a mainstay in our message, and it should be. But we erroneously overlook Christ's practice of linking the Good News to our Kingdom citizenship. The gospel is not merely indicative of where we are headed; it determines our identity. We are—present tense—ambassadors of a heavenly Kingdom, and we are to live on earth according to the Kingdom's culture. Christ, our King, said, "The time has come. . . . The kingdom of God has come near. Repent and believe the good news!" (Mark 1:15). For Christ, the Kingdom of God and the good news are invariably linked. It is why devotion to him should be upheld by our material impact in a broken world. Our citizenship should be evident (Matthew 25:31-46).

To claim the salvation of the Lord while remaining stagnant is an insult to the one who paid the grand price for our wholeness. But we are never without hope; it is the reason

I can remain an evangelical. It is never too late to return to our first love (Revelation 2:4) and become uncompromising arbiters of Christ's accomplishment. After centuries of escorting passengers to lifeboats, I pray we turn our gospel prowess to the ship's restoration. It is a Kingdom act—fruits of a comprehensive gospel.

6

THE POWER OF PROXIMITY

Jonathan Brooks

ONE SUNDAY I hurried around the corner to open the door for our morning gathering at Canaan Community Church in Chicago because I needed to prepare for Sunday school. As I walked up, I noticed there was a man waiting at the door. Although it is not strange to have neighbors or other residents join us from the community, we rarely have anyone waiting outside for us to open. I was in a hurry, and although I am always glad to meet new people, I was not particularly excited to see him this morning. I picked up my pace to meet him at the door and find out what he needed.

When Confronted with Needs

When confronted with the needs around us, it is easy to view the least of these as "less than," to turn away, or to cross the street to avoid interacting with those who are shunned.

We Often View Others as Less Than

As I took the last few steps toward the man on the church steps, he turned around, looked at me, and said, "Hey, do you know the pastor of this church?" Once again it was not strange for people to meet me and assume that the pastor was a little older and probably not wearing dreadlocks, jeans, and Air Jordan gym shoes. I responded, "Yeah, I know him. I can introduce you to him if you like." As I reached out my hand to shake his, I said, "I am Pastor Jonathan Brooks, but everybody calls me Pastah J." He smiled and responded, "My name is Ivan, and I was wondering if I could ask you something." If I am being honest, I was automatically thinking that what was coming next was a request for money, food, housing, or help with some other need. Ivan was not dressed poorly, nor did he necessarily look like he lacked money, food, or housing, yet I immediately jumped to the conclusion that he needed something from me. I had already placed him in a less than position; I viewed myself as the service provider and him as the service recipient.

In Mark 5:25-34 we read of a woman who is healed from a hemorrhage that had been going on continuously for twelve years. This story displays the power of proximity and the amazing faith of a woman who was in desperate need of Jesus' healing power. But we must also reflect on the context of this story to gain insight into its implications. Mark 5:26 says, "She had suffered a great deal under the care of many doctors and had spent all she had, yet instead of getting better she grew worse." Due to her hemorrhaging, this woman was considered ceremonially unclean and was on the outside of the community. Once she had tapped all her financial and relational resources, her situation went from bleak to hopeless. The woman's physical illness was made even more difficult by her "less than" social status. Being seen as less than and on the margins likely caused her to feel like she had nothing to lose, so she decided to pursue this Jesus she had heard about. She probably figured since no one else had helped thus far, she might as well try to repair her situation on her own. If she could just touch the edge of Jesus' clothes, she believed, she would be made well (verse 28).

This woman's position in society as "unclean" and poor is what determined her care—or, more accurately, lack of care—by the community and by the religious leaders of her day. When people are viewed as less than, whether by the community or the church, it exacerbates any societal issues they may already be experiencing.

We Often Turn Away

As I conversed with Ivan, he opened up about his past issues with addiction and his current path of sobriety and stability. What he wanted from me was not a handout but a hand up. He asked if he could connect with our congregation because he had learned in his recovery group that he needed to be linked to something greater than himself. Ivan confessed that he had lost contact with his family due to his behavior while still in his addiction and had no one he could count on to be there for him. After listening to him for a few minutes, I was completely humbled and humiliated. If I had turned away from Ivan due to my busyness or my incorrect judgment of him, I would have not only missed an opportunity for myself but also caused my congregation to miss a God-ordained relationship.

Before Jesus' encounter with the bleeding woman, he had recently crossed back over the Sea of Galilee after a chaotic experience with a man he healed from demon possession. He has just stepped off the boat when a synagogue leader named Jairus asks him to heal his daughter so that she might live, and Jesus agrees. While he is on his way to heal the little girl, the bleeding woman approaches him. The disciples are trying to get Jesus through the town, and a large crowd is following him and pressing in on him. There are many people around Jesus with needs, but he is focused on the other good work he has set out to do. He does not initially notice the woman and her need, until she touches him.

This is not because Jesus is mean, arrogant, or self-centered but simply because he is already on a mission. While we cannot ignore the fact that Jesus does not initially see this woman or acknowledge her condition, it is important to recognize that he is just passing through on his way to heal someone else. We must remember that there were many people who lived in this place who had seen her needs repeatedly but turned away. The question we must ask ourselves is *In what ways have we turned away from people around us every day, causing them to be in a desperate situation where their only choice is to seek a miracle from Jesus?*

We Often Avoid Interactions

When encountering people like Ivan, it's often easy for us to view them as an interruption to avoid rather than an invitation to accept. Jesus' disciples, often out of necessity, specialized in avoidance, and their reaction to the woman with a hemorrhage in our story was no different.

As our passage continues in Mark 5:27-28, the disciples are trying to protect Jesus from the crowds of people around him. They are attempting to get him from point A to point B with as little resistance as possible. The woman is determined to get as close to Jesus as possible because she had heard about him and believed if she could just touch the edge of his robe, she would be healed. I can imagine this woman literally crawling on her hands and knees, reaching between the legs of the people in this huge crowd just to touch the edge of his robe. Then the disciples suddenly hear Jesus say, "Somebody touched me." Thinking he is being irrational, they reply, "Teacher, there are many people touching you!" (verses 30-31, author's paraphrase). But Jesus needs them to understand that this wasn't just an accidental jostling from someone in the crowd. This was the kind of touch that had interrupted his established agenda and could not be avoided.

Prior to when she had grabbed the edge of his robe, Jesus had not noticed this woman or her situation even though he had the resources she needed. It was her faith and pursuit of him that affected him. When we intentionally move toward the marginalized around us, the perceived interruptions we typically try to avoid become invitations for us to accept. Through these interactions we can be touched by stories of faith, humility, and joy. In his book *Turn My Mourning into Dancing*, Henri Nouwen wrote of a priest who told him, "I have always been complaining that my work was constantly interrupted; then I realized that the interruptions were my work."[1]

How Compassion Is Developed

Compassion is developed through personal interaction. What can we do to put ourselves in proximity to and relationship with those we are often tempted to ignore?

Personal Proximity

After our Sunday-morning study time, Ivan stayed for our worship experience. All our church members who had been there kept remarking to those coming in for worship how amazing the study had been that morning. They kept introducing Ivan to people as they walked through the door, and Ivan seemed to be just as excited to get to know as many members as he could. Our worship time was powerful and meaningful as we sang together, prayed together, and pondered together on how Jesus had led Ivan to our church door that morning in search of the body of Christ that Paul describes in 1 Corinthians 12. We didn't know Ivan, nor did we know the depths of his story, but just being close to him and his tremendous faith in God had already begun to change our church in ways we had not yet comprehended.

In order to discuss my favorite part of the story in Mark 5 we need to go back a few verses to discuss the moment the woman is healed (verse 29). I love that all this woman has to do to be healed is to *get in proximity to Jesus*. He isn't even aware that she is close to him or that she is counting on him to make this miracle happen. As soon as the woman gets close to Jesus, her hemorrhage immediately stops, and she feels in her body that she is healed. If Jesus hadn't been in her vicinity or approximate to her physical location, this miracle wouldn't have taken place.

Now, we know that Jesus can miraculously heal without being in the same geographical location as the person with physical needs. This is proven when he heals the centurion's servant without ever going to his bedside (Luke 7:1-10). But how is the healing *we* can provide possible when we aren't even aware of the needs around us? Jesus needed people in proximity to the problem to tell him about it. There are stories in Scripture where people who are sick or physically disabled are brought to Jesus because they can't get to him themselves. In Mark 2:1-12, we see four men tear a hole in a roof and lower their paralyzed friend on a stretcher to get him in proximity to Jesus, believing that he would heal him.

To get the paralyzed man close to Jesus, these men had to be close to him first.

When we are not in proximity to those in need, not only are we unable to meet their needs, but we may be unable to even *see* their needs. This marginalized woman is able to make her way to Jesus even though society and the religious leaders had failed to get in proximity to her. Due to her resiliency and perseverance, the woman gets close to Jesus and her needs are met. The community members and religious leaders around her missed the opportunity to be in proximity themselves. They were so enamored with the sight of Jesus that they missed the opportunity to be like Jesus.

Personal Interaction

Ivan became a committed member of our congregation. We spent the next few months really growing together in every way. I learned from him the true struggles of addiction and what a powerful man he truly was to have overcome so much. He helped me to see God, the Scriptures, and even my position as his pastor in new ways. It seemed that whenever I needed a word of encouragement or a prayer, Ivan would call or show up at the church just to encourage me. I walked alongside him while he found work and then made sure he got to work consistently and on time. As a congregation, we helped organize his finances, open his first bank account, and then move out of the halfway house he'd been living in and into his own apartment. Through the good days and bad, Ivan was as committed to being there for me as I was for him.

Once the bleeding woman touches Jesus, he has to pause what he's doing and find out who she is. When he stops in his tracks and exclaims, "Somebody touched me," the woman knows she can no longer hide and admits it was her. What happens next is such a powerful personal interaction. After being healed of this issue she's had for twelve years, the woman looks at Jesus, in fear and trembling, and tells him the whole truth. Why was she afraid? Well, the power dynamics here were not in her favor. Jesus was a well-known Jewish man with God-given healing powers, and she was an "unclean" poor woman who shouldn't have touched him, according to rules of her culture. Due to her societal status, this interaction could have gone wrong quickly, and in her mind, Jesus had every right to be upset with her or even to dismiss her. But Jesus doesn't dismiss her; instead, he honors her faith by speaking directly to her publicly amid this large crowd. He also tells her that her faith has made her well.

Jesus loves and desires personal interaction with all people. If we want to develop genuine compassion in our own lives, we, too, must seek personal relationships, especially with those typically considered the least of these. Imagine what might happen if we weren't so busy with our personal agendas and appointments that we allowed the stories of the marginalized to stop us in our tracks. What if we allowed them to affect us in ways we couldn't ignore? This could be the beginning of beautiful relationships that extend far beyond simply meeting each other's needs—starting with personal interactions where we truly meet one another.

Personal Relationship

Due to continuous proximity and personal interaction, my relationship with Ivan has matured significantly. It has been a joy to walk with him as he's met many of the goals he shared with me on the steps of the church years ago. We have laughed together, cried together, and discussed some of the most intimate parts of our lives with each other. Ivan has surpassed friend status; he has truly become my brother. We rejoiced together when he got a job with full benefits at a renowned hospital, something he thought would never happen. I remember the first time he brought his then fiancée, Velda, to church so everyone there could meet her. Now they are married, and I had the honor of officiating their wedding. Ivan has also been supportive, even as I have transitioned to my new pastoral position at Lawndale Christian Community Church. Ivan has a dream of working with men in recovery, and through the partnership of the two churches, he's been connected with one of the founders of Lawndale's Hope House ministry. Hope House has been serving men coming out of prison and/or off drugs or alcohol for nearly three decades.

In Mark 5:34, Jesus says to the woman, "Daughter, your faith has healed you. Go in peace and be freed from your suffering." What I absolutely love is the way that Jesus addresses this woman. Prior to this moment she has been cast out, viewed as less than, and shunned by the people of her community, and now by the crowd that has formed around Jesus. But once the woman is in proximity to Jesus and has a personal interaction with him, he refers to her as "daughter." What happens here is we see Jesus engaging with the woman relationally. She is now a daughter whose faith has healed and freed her from her suffering. Jesus is so touched by this woman's faith that he stops, looks her in the eye, addresses her as daughter, and then blesses her on the rest of her journey. This is not done privately but publicly. Everyone who was in proximity to this miracle was amazed and saw the power of God working through Jesus. Even someone who wasn't present but who came in contact with this woman had a testimony and example of the power of God working through Jesus. She was a walking billboard for what Jesus could do for anyone who had faith in him and who he claimed to be. This is the desired result of our proximity and presence with the least of these: that we might gain relationship with them in ways that change us both.

Her proximity to and personal interaction with Jesus begins a mutually beneficial relationship where Jesus is no longer just the service provider but—through her faith and testimony—becomes a recipient as well. Her public narrative, "I was sick, I touched Jesus, and now I'm healed," also helps his private ministry. Ultimately, Jesus can teach another lesson about his power: that it can be activated by faith. The crowds saw what happened and his disciples did as well.

We Are Meant to Help Each Other

Like me when I saw Ivan on the church steps that Sunday morning, the temptation to ignore the needs of those around is very real. As human beings, we have an inbred capacity to take care of ourselves, as well as physical reactions that make us feel good about ourselves when we help someone, even if only from a distance. Real compassion, however, is when we enter into mutually beneficial opportunities with our neighbors through personal proximity, personal interactions, and personal relationships. What we find when we re-examine our views on compassion is that we are meant to help each other. In fact, we are also meant to be with each other. Whenever we find ourselves in one-way relationships in which there is no mutual benefit, then we likely aren't practicing compassion but rather a form of patronization that is meant to make us feel good about ourselves. This is not the Kingdom at all.

Real compassion not only meets needs caused by social ills but works alongside those most marginalized by society to devise solutions. Therefore, the Kingdom conversation has to go beyond the meeting of needs caused by marginalization. It has to move into the realm of relational engagement that causes us to desire the eradication of all marginalization in the world. Personal proximity, personal interactions, and personal relationships are what eventually move our Kingdom conversations from simply compassion—which is defined as "sympathetic consciousness of others' distress together with a desire to alleviate it"[2]—toward conversations about the pursuit of what is just, which means "acting or being in conformity with what is morally upright or good."[3] If we pay close attention to the two definitions, we see that compassion focuses on our *concern for* suffering, while justice focuses on our *response to* suffering. In his poem titled "Is Justice Worth It?" poet and rapper Micah Bournes says it this way:

Is [justice] even worth it? . . . That question . . . rarely comes from people who have labored for years and have good reason to ask it. And, you know why they never ask? Those type of people become friends with those who suffer. Family, even. Because it is one thing to wonder if someone else is worth fighting for, but when you begin to identify with that someone else, commune with them—that's when the question is no longer worth asking. That's when it becomes offensive, even. What do you *mean* is it worth my time? That doesn't even deserve an answer. I don't care how long it takes. I don't care how many times we fail. I don't care how little progress is made. You *never* stop fighting for your own.[4]

7

A CALL FOR A MULTI-ABILITY CHURCH

Daniel Aaron Harris

I WAS BORN WITH CEREBRAL PALSY. Because of damage to my brain, I can't make my hands or my limbs do what I want them to do.[1]

For most of my life, I believed that in order to be part of the body of Christ, I needed to be made completely whole—and I had the wrong idea of what "whole" was going to be. That was partly because of what I was taught in the church where I grew up. That church was part of the charismatic movement, in which there was a lot of talk about being healed and completely made whole. As a result, I believed that I had to be just like everybody else, with a whole body, to be a part of the body in community.

But about five years ago, I began to work through a theology of disability. It started with a conversation with a friend of mine. I asked: "Will I be like this in heaven? How did God make me? Did God make me the way I am? If so, then why?"

This conversation took me into my own journey of exploring what it means to have a disability and be a Christian. And I realized that disability is not just a thing that some people experience. Disability—limitations and weakness—are part of being human.

A Gospel of Humanity

For me, in my church, there was a time when I felt like an awkward outsider who didn't fit into the body of Christ. I thought that the gospel suggested I had to be whole—as in, a whole different person—but that's simply not true.

God made it clear to me: *You are not a creature who nobody wants to be around; you are part of my body. I created you just as you are. Not only did I create you, but I love the way you walk. I love the way you talk.* At one time, that was a hard thing for me to grasp, but that is because I didn't know the whole gospel. I was only looking at my own perspective. I didn't have a real picture of why Jesus came. I needed to know why Jesus came for me—just as well as why he came for you.

To understand the gospel, we have to understand what it means to be human. John 1 says that God became a human in order to come and die for us. God *gave away power* to became human. In addition to being poor and marginalized, he became *dis-abled* on earth so that he could die for us. And then, dying on the cross, Jesus was dis-abled in an unjust way. He didn't deserve it; he did it for us. As theology professor Nancy Eiesland wrote:

> In the resurrected Jesus Christ, they saw not the suffering servant for whom the last and most important word was tragedy and sin, but the disabled God who embodied both impaired hands and feet and pierced side and the imago Dei. Paradoxically, in the very act commonly understood as the transcendence of physical life, God is revealed as tangible, bearing the representation of the body reshaped by injustice and sin into the fullness of the Godhead.[2]

When we celebrate at the Lord's Table, we talk about the blood of Jesus Christ, and we talk about how the bread represents the broken body. This idea of Jesus' body being broken for me tells me that God knows what it means to have a disability. God knows what it's like to walk around in a body with limitations. In Hebrews 2:14-18, we see that Jesus became "fully human in every way" (verse 17). He did this to die and to free us from the penalty of sin, but this also means that he knows what we go through.

If we don't look at disability, we are missing out on the whole of human experience. Humanity involves all of us. That is one of the reasons why so many people are afraid to talk about disability: It is the one people group that we are all part of, and we don't want to think about that. Instead, we marginalize whole groups of people with disabilities. We do the same thing with other groups of people who are unfamiliar or uncomfortable for us: the poor, the sick, those of different ethnicities—people on the margins.

A Kingdom Enability Model

When I look at what it means to be redeemed by the blood, I realize God is not only saving me from my own sin but also from the sins of people around me. God is also redeeming who I am as a man and who I am as a human, and he uses me to bring redemption to the world. Knowing this, we can move toward developing a practical theology of disability, what I call a Kingdom Enability model. In this model based on Scripture, *everyone*—even those with disability or otherwise on the margins—is created, connected, called, and commissioned.

1. **We are created.** We are all created in God's image just as we are (Genesis 1:26; Psalm 139:13). The Fall did not change the fact that we are God's handiwork (Ephesians 2:10). God made man in his own image, and he had a relationship with Adam and Eve—he was in community with humans. When Adam sinned, it was about the relationship being marred, not about the body or mind being marred.

2. **We are connected.** We are all connected to one another in Christ. As Paul writes to the church at Corinth, "We were all baptized by one Spirit so as to form one body—whether Jews or Gentiles, slave or free—and we were all given the one Spirit to drink" (1 Corinthians 12:13).

3. **We are called.** All of us have been called according to God's purpose into "one body and one Spirit" (Ephesians 4:4) and to a holy life, "not because of anything we have done but because of his own purpose and grace" (2 Timothy 1:9). Calling is not unique to the nondisabled or to those in societal positions of power.

4. **We are commissioned.** As followers of Christ, we are all commissioned to fulfill the great commission to "Go and make disciples of all nations" (Matthew 28:19). Just because I have a disability doesn't let me off the hook. *All* of us have been given the great commission.

With these four Cs, we have to remember that everything in the Bible should be carried out and viewed by all parties the same. Therefore, these statements are true for people with outward physical disabilities as well as those with inward and hidden disabilities. Every one of us has an obligation of service for God's Kingdom. The "go" will just look different for each person based on our gifts and context.

Kathleen Cahalan's book *Introducing the Practice of Ministry* defines two kinds of vocation. A general vocation is being a disciple of Christ. A calling or ministerial vocation is a specific thing you are designed to do. She writes, "Vocation is a life lived in response to the following questions: Who I am? How do I live? What service do I offer to the world?"[3]

As an artist and author, part of my vocation is writing and illustrating children's books. It is a unique way to show not only who *I* am but what others can be. Dr. Seuss said, "A person's a person, no matter how small."[4] Dr. Seuss wrote for people of all ages, but he also knew that kids grow up into adults. Through my children's books I can help guide a different narrative for people with disabilities.

Vocation Rooted in Location

Turning to Scripture, and more specifically the Pauline Epistles, we see a clear example of how "Go" looks different for everyone depending on location. Paul's location had great influence on his ministerial vocation. Paul writes to the Galatians, "It was because of a bodily ailment that I preached the gospel to you at first" (Galatians 4:13, ESV). Even while imprisoned, Paul made a point of ministering out of his location and writing specific letters to different communities, including the Galatians, Philippians, and Colossians. Every one of us has a ministerial vocation that is rooted in location, no matter our level of physical ability.

One of my biggest influences has been a man named Ray Bakke. Growing up in rural America, Bakke came from a family of dairy farmers and loggers. By the time he was a young adult, he knew that God had another plan for his life. Bakke moved to Chicago to attend Moody Bible Institute and started a journey of learning about the city. Bakke believed that in order to minister to a city, you must become part of it and learn from it. He wrote:

> We can look at any place in London or Chicago as sacred because God is present and at work there. We can also look at any place as sacred to which we are called as Christians and in which we minister for Christ. We cannot work in our city unless we love it—its architecture, sewer system, politics, history, traditions, and neighborhoods.[5]

If there is any way that I'm going to minister the gospel, I need to understand the mindset and the reason why Memphis is the way it is. I was born and raised in Memphis, and the blues are in my blood. The blues are a musical expression that evokes emotion in the same way as a poem, a film, or a play. The listener is a participant, invited to understand something. Living in Memphis has affected how I do what I do. As I live out my life and my faith on a daily basis, I have the opportunity for a ministry of evocative presence—of inviting others to understand and respond—simply by being and doing.

Using this model of the four Cs, I believe we can begin to see true wholeness and transformation take place. This is a Kingdom-enabled practical theology that sets all people free.

The Church's Response

This model can help cast a new vision for a multi-ability church. The body of Christ must develop a better practical theology of ministry *from* and not just *to* the margins.

We must start by examining the prominent leadership styles that we see today. Many contemporary leadership styles have their origin in the Industrial Revolution, in which the dominant mindset was, as theologian and professor John Swinton describes:

> If you cannot keep up and use your time
> productively, you will become an economic and
> social burden on the state, on your family, and on
> society; you will become a "handicap" to process,
> a drag on the desired forward movement of society
> within which everyone is expected to strive to create
> their own personal history.[6]

Here we see how the world is identifying us based on what we can do rather than who we are. Various current leadership models enforce this identification process. Is this why people on the margins are not in church leadership roles? Is it because we have allowed the worldly leadership philosophies to seep into the church? If so, a practical theology of disability should consider worldly leadership culture and its effect on church culture.

Many churches have also bought into a false gospel. Growing up, I was taught that if I believed in Jesus, I should have health and wealth. When this becomes normalized theology, it can drive people to ignore or hide their weaknesses.

In addition, we must examine our assumptions about people on the margins. All too often they are associated with sin or sinful choices, and it may be further argued that they have no agency over their own body. Remember the question Jesus' disciples asked him about the man blind from birth: "Rabbi, who sinned, this man or his parents, that he was born blind?" (John 9:2). But as we have seen earlier, disability is a part of humanity, and you are a holy being because you are human.

Amanda Leduc's *Disfigured: On Fairy Tales, Disability, and Making Space* examines the way we portray disability in society. She talks about how disability in stories much of the time is the result of sloppy writing. This is why we receive characters like Captain Hook from *Peter Pan* and Scar from *The Lion King*. We know as an audience that the guy with a hook is a bad guy and the lion with a scar is a bad guy; it is a simple way to tell a story. Leduc argues we should dig more into our stories and discover new ways of making the bad guy a real bad guy without a mark.[7]

The reason why culture does this so often in stories is not new. The stories are validating cultural ideologies. On the other hand, Victor Hugo's *Hunchback of Notre-Dame* tells a story about a hunchback named Quasimodo. Quasimodo is not portrayed as the bad guy but rather as a protector of the church. Living in the bell tower, Quasimodo has many different meanings behind his character.[8]

Once we shed our false beliefs, we can begin to cast a new vision for the church. Books like Kathy Black's *A Healing Homiletic* and others can transform the way we interpret the biblical narrative. This starts when we stop looking at the people in Gospel healing stories as subjects and instead see them as human beings. Black argues that we need to transform the way we perceive healing. "When cure is not currently possible, healing can happen through the supportive, accepting community; through our own ability (undergirded by God's strength and the support of others) to make it through the hard times; and through the different, new possibilities that are open for us," she writes.[9]

Healing can also look like giving someone a voice or inviting them to be part of the community. We must realize how connected we are in order to see a community working together with each person's vocation. We are all one in the body. If we come to realize the truth of the four Cs, we can then participate, cultivate, and activate everyone around us.

First, we *participate* by caring and by learning from each other's communities. Second, we *cultivate* by loving, encouraging, and supporting the gifts inside each other in the ways of Jesus Christ in order to see the whole body of Christ built up. Third, we *activate*, sending each other out in the world to proclaim the gospel using the unique vocation and gifts God has given each of us.

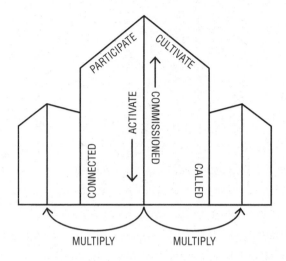

Yet a biblical model that transforms the structure *inside* the church isn't enough. We must be a prophetic demonstration to those communities in which we live. Youth With A Mission's "Seven Spheres of Influence" provides a helpful framework. When people are plugged in based on their gifts to the areas of family, religion/church, education, government, media, celebration (arts, entertainment, and sports), and economics (business, science, and technology), flourishing will take place.[10] In this way, we *multiply* our impact beyond the walls of the church.

Growing up, I always wanted to fit in a certain ministry role, but much like Leduc writes, I couldn't picture myself in the stories or roles that society and the church provided. But what if I didn't have to? What if—like Quasimodo's bell tower—there is a place in the church for true complexity of

Christian character formation? Instead of fitting into a preset model, we should invent our own. The gospel never changes, but methods do. If we are all created, connected, called, and commissioned, then it is incumbent on us all to change those methods.

The Blues for the Body of Christ

The blues originated from the Black experience in America and can be traced back to slavery. It's a way to cope with various kinds of oppressions through musical expression. But are the blues only musical? In an interview, Cornel West defined the blues as "an autobiographical chronicle of a personal catastrophe expressed lyrically and endured with grace and dignity. Meaning what? Meaning that the blues are all those who are willing to look unflinchingly at catastrophic conditions."[11] If you really listen to the blues, many of the songs are a call-and-response, much like the liturgy of church services that have a call to worship and a congregational response to that call.

With this terminology in mind, the blues can be birthed out of any experience. How does a person on the margins "sing the blues"? Can I, as a man with cerebral palsy, express my oppression in order to love my church and my city well? I have found my "blues song" within my own passions. Through self-discovery I've found that by becoming an artist, author, and actor, I'm able to sing my blues song, thus loving my city and congregation well.

Or what if, instead of thinking solely in terms of

geographic place, we use the Kingdom Enability model to think of each person as a place? That would mean that each of us—created, connected, called, and commissioned—tell our stories to each other.

Marginalized people need to tell what is going on now and what has gone on before so we can begin singing a song for the future. The blues is more than music; it's experiences and how we articulate those experiences. As people of God, we need to proclaim our experiences to those in our larger communities so that we can all experience truth. This is what, in my observation, the blues men and women were doing. So go grab a pencil, a paintbrush, a guitar, and proclaim that experience. We all need you to sing your blues song.

And then, what is the congregational, communal response to that song? As a man with cerebral palsy, the reason why I'm celebrating my eighteenth year of ministry is that people around me helped me become a disciple of Jesus. When we do this on a large scale with a multi-ability church in mind, we will begin the manifestation of Christ's body on earth.

8

WHAT CAN WE DO?

Danielle Strickland

THIS IS THE QUESTION. We live in a time when exposure to injustice is everywhere. If you wanted to avoid the awkward uncertainty of injustice or the blazing oppression of evil raging everywhere around the world right now, you'd have to live in a cave. The sheer enormity of the waves of need and wrong are overwhelming to absorb, let alone to try to change. So, what can we do?

We Lament

That's where we begin. The activist in me is angry that I've just typed these words. *Don't do that*, I tell myself. *You are letting everyone off the hook.* But God in his mercy took me back to a time when I was paralyzed with the onslaught of deep need. I had landed in a neighborhood given over to despair. I regularly walked by people with a drug addiction in full stupor in the alley outside my apartment. I saw the oppressive cycle of human trafficking and the unjust living conditions of people stuck experiencing constant rejection. I raged against it.

One day, I was prayer walking through the neighborhood with my partner in ministry. I was waxing eloquent about the plans I had to change things. I picked up my pace to get to fixing things, setting things right, changing the world. But when I turned to look for an affirming nod, my prayer partner was no longer with me. Bewildered, I looked around and saw her out of the corner of my eye. She was kneeling at the feet of the first addict we had seen. She had covered her half-naked body with her coat and was on her knees—weeping. Just weeping. I rolled my eyes (internally, of course) at the waste of emotion when we could channel our energy in more meaningful ways. A shelter, a drop-in center, adequate housing, proper treatment, and those things would come. But they wouldn't come first. First, we would weep.

Shortly after this frustrating experience, God showed me the prophetic example of Ezekiel. It takes two chapters of the book to explain, but let me summarize (Ezekiel 8–9). God, by his Spirit, takes Ezekiel by the hair of his head and shows him the sins of Israel. So much sin that Ezekiel asks him to stop, but God declines. He needs him to see it all. God tells Ezekiel that he is looking for people who will weep and mourn for the sins of Israel. He's sending an angel to mark the foreheads of all who will weep. It will set them apart. It will save them from death. Weeping. Mourning. Wow.

God was revealing that before anything can change *externally*, things need to change *internally*. It's not just what we do that matters, but why and how we do it. God has a power greater than and different from the power that is at work in this world. And the way to access that power, to be set apart by God to participate in his Kingdom coming, is through a soft and broken heart.

Maybe that's why World Vision founder Bob Pierce's simple prayer has the power and potency to create global advocacy and mercy around the world. "Let my heart be broken with the things that break the heart of God,"[1] he wrote. Might that be the place we begin? Jesus put it much more simply: "Blessed are the poor in spirit. . . . Blessed are those who mourn. . . . Blessed are the meek" (Matthew 5:3-5). All the things that look opposite to a blessed life are the way to participate in the life of Jesus.

We Stand against Evil

The weeping helps us shave the calluses that form over our hearts and in our minds. That hardness, if it isn't dealt with, ends up twisting us into the ways and shape of the enemy. It's from the soft place—our broken spirit, our open heart—that we take our stand against evil schemes.

The apostle Paul tells us straight, "We do not wrestle against flesh and blood" (Ephesians 6:12, NKJV). This is a complicated truth. The easiest and most tempting action is to pick human enemies and to stand against them. A woman on the receiving end of male violence can easily assume her fight is against men. BIPOC leaders who have suffered from racist policies and systems perpetuated by whiteness can quickly identify white people as the enemy. Global neighbors who suffer from hunger and watch the Western world live in excess can easily identify their enemy as us. Survivors of war can see their enemy in a human form as they fire their guns and destroy their homes. We identify our enemy, and then we stand against them. And this is why a broken and soft heart is so essential. Because to truly fight as the children of God and with the Spirit of God, to take a real stand against injustice, we must fight in the strength and power of God. And that power is not just *greater* than but *different* from the power of this world.

Paul helps us identify our true enemy, and this is essential if we are to push back the forces of evil behind the deep injustices and oppression of this age. Our true fight is with the principalities and powers of darkness. They manifest themselves through violence, abuse, war, racism, misogyny, patriarchy, extreme poverty, colonialism, exploitation, broken systems and structures, disordered principles and ideas. But to state it once again, we do not fight against flesh and blood. We take our stand against the evil forces *behind* them. This cannot be overemphasized.

When we identify our real enemy, we can understand how to fight back. To misidentify our true enemy is to succumb to the strategy of darkness. In an increasingly polarized world, this is essential for us to grasp. It's also the only hope of potentially making any difference. Activism and mercy that does not operate from the power of God will only make things worse. Recently, through some close encounters with clergy sexual abuse in my own church, I've become keenly aware of the temptation to fight against flesh and blood. The anger that seeks revenge instead of restoration rages. But I refuse it. Instead, I weep. And then I stand. I stand against the power of darkness. And I combat that power with the power of God. This power that God gives us is not just greater than the powers and principalities of this world but different from them as well.

This point has grown more essential for me to explain than ever before. We sing triumphant worship songs that flex God's power all the time. "Our God is greater; our God is stronger,"[2] and I believe them. Except I wish we'd add a line like "Our God's power is *different* from all the others." In our world-shaped minds, we tend to imagine God's power as a stronger version of the others. As though God is a greater pharaoh or a more powerful caesar. But then we miss the main point of the power of God at work in this world. We miss the essential truth that God's power is not just greater but *different as well*. I genuinely believe that I may have misunderstood the power of God because of my saturation and hunger for the power of this world. But they are so very different from each other. And maybe you were hoping for a more practical list of things we can do to fight against the injustice and suffering of our world. But I'm convinced that without this understanding of power, all our work will be in vain.

The power that God gives is not like the power of empire, conquest, or control. It is not a worldly kind of power. Its distinguishing features are too many to list, but the fact that it is freely given isn't a bad place to start. It is not controlling; it liberates. It is not a power "over" but a power "under." The Spirit of Jesus will not possess but partner. The power of God will send followers out with instructions to freely give that power away! The power of God infuses people with the desire for justice and enables followers to stand in solidarity with those who are oppressed. The power of God will enable leaders to give up their rights for others. The power of God will lead us to crucifixion and death if it will help demonstrate what love looks like in an oppressive world. God's power is openhanded, not closedfisted. God's power is others-focused, not self-absorbed. To distinguish God's power from the power and principalities at work in and through this world is essential to steward it well. Our track record here is abysmal, so I think it's worth reviewing.

Recently I was thinking about the power of God as demonstrated through the book of Acts. I was remembering that incredible moment when the apostles were imprisoned. God's power caused an earthquake to break the doors open, and the apostles were free to leave (Acts 16:25-40). But they didn't. And here is where the real power begins to show up. The power of God was only beginning its work through the earthquake. The real work, the real power, was manifested through the actions of the apostles in the decision they made to *stay in jail* even though they could go free. It is so unfathomable for me to comprehend. *Run, apostles, run!* is what I think when I read this story. But the power at work within them was for saving people, not escaping pain. So, when they saw that their jailer was afraid that he and his family would die because he allowed them to escape—they stayed. They stayed for him and his family. They stayed in prison for their jailer's life. That's the power of God. I pray God will infuse us with this kind of power. Because this power will help us identify our true enemy. And the hint from this text is simply this: The enemy is not a person.

Identifying our real enemy also helps us invite people to fight with us against a common foe. It's this spirit that drove Martin Luther King Jr. to refuse the ideology that he was fighting against white people. He understood clearly that he was fighting against racism and invited everyone to be free from its evil grip. He wrote, "Whatever affects one directly, affects all indirectly. . . . I can never be what I ought to be until you are what you ought to be. And you can never be what you ought to be until I am what I ought to be—this is the interrelated structure of reality."[3]

King understood that God's liberating power would set us all free together. Archbishop Desmond Tutu said it like this: "When we see others as the enemy, we risk becoming what we hate. When we oppress others, we end up oppressing ourselves. All of our humanity is dependent on recognizing the humanity in others."[4]

It's this truth that runs through the life and witness of Jesus and the early church. It's this kind of power that can set both the oppressed and the oppressor free from the darkness that threatens to consume them both.

The power of God is manifested in truth, love, and life. Once we have taken a stand against our true enemy, we use these divine strategies to fight back.

We Replace Lies with Truth

The enemy's language is lies. And by lies I mean not only the kind that are whispered in the dark, but also the shadowy fog that insists on things being too complicated for us to really understand. Anywhere there is an absence of light the enemy is at work.

So, to fight against evil in all its forms, we walk in the light.

Now, it sounds like a catchy song (cue DC Talk[5]), but it's also a potent and powerful weapon to push back evil. The light. The darkness can't stand it—and those who like the darkness will often refuse it. At the entrance of Jesus into this world, the writer of John's Gospel explains, "This is the verdict: Light has come into the world, but people loved darkness instead of light because their deeds were evil" (John 3:19).

Walking in the light is getting informed about the truth and then telling it. It is caring enough about the injustice that you seek to understand. It is getting curious and continuing to ask disruptive questions, even when people don't want you to. Don't stop. Keep asking, and keep seeking truth.

Drag whatever darkness you find into the light. Not just outside of you but also inside of you. We can never separate the oppression we fight *against* from the oppression we fight *within*. Theologian and civil rights leader Howard Thurman explains it like this: "Again and again, I am aware that the Light not only illumines but it also *burns*."[6]

The light outside and the light inside are always connected. That's what makes the light such a potent and powerful weapon.

We Replace Fear with Love

The enemy uses a currency of fear. Nonviolence leader Mohandas Gandhi once explained, "The enemy is fear. We think it is hate; but it is really fear." Fear is the means by which the enemy keeps everyone locked into oppressive cycles. Reread the story of the tyrannical pharaoh who ordered the mass murder of Israelite baby boys in Exodus, and you will discover he did it because he was afraid (Exodus 1:10). Fear is a powerful and demonic motivator, and we've all been on a steady diet of fear for a long while.

But there is a greater power that can overcome fear—it's love.[7] Love is the currency of the Kingdom. It's the way God moves. It's the motive for what God does. It's the power that unleashes hope and peace into this world. Now, even as I say "love," you might get a little nervous. Most likely you understand love as sentimental feelings of goodness toward other people. You might think of love as a little, well, soft. But I assure you that the power of God's love is a force, an authority, a way of ushering in freedom and future. Dr. Cornel West warns us, "Never forget that justice is what love looks like in public."[8]

And I agree. Love is a currency that ushers in truth and stands in solidarity with the oppressed. Love is both disruptive and casts out fear at the same time. I'm often baffled by the image of Jesus driving the money lenders out of the Temple, turning over the tables. And in the same story the text continues, "The blind and the lame came to him at the temple, and he healed them" (Matthew 21:14).

Love leads us toward the other; the enemy separates. Love humanizes; the enemy dehumanizes. Love moves toward; the enemy moves away. Love embraces; the enemy excludes. Love is hospitable; the enemy isolates. Love forgives and restores; the enemy excuses and ignores. Love moves people to repentance; the enemy justifies their wrongs. Love is curious and open; the enemy is certain and closed. And this goes on and on and on. Love is the only power potent enough to liberate us from the grip of evil. If you truly want to do something to combat injustice and evil, learn to live and work and fight in love. As author and teacher Bradley Jersak writes, "Christ commands us to love our enemies and to overcome evil with good. He calls us to make love our first allegiance—and his love *frees* us to do so. Freedom in Christ, ironically, is freedom from the tyranny of our own paranoia-producing self-will and fear-driven self-preservation, which we've tragically mislabeled 'freedom.'"[9]

We Replace Separation and Death with Connection and Life

Jesus tells us very clearly that the enemy has come to steal, kill, and destroy (John 10:10). That's what he does. That is his aim. Sometimes when I think about injustice, I'm baffled by it. It seems to make no sense at all. And then Jesus reminds me that it destroys and it steals and it kills, and that's all the sense the enemy needs. It's what evil wants. Think about it.

All the injustices you've read about so far and the ones that keep you up at night. The millions and millions of kids stuck in refugee camps struggling with trauma and separation from their families, the sheer ridiculousness of war and its result—destruction and death. The enormous amount of money being made by companies raping and pillaging the earth for personal gain and doing what? Destroying, stealing, killing our future, our hopes, our climate, our world. Why?

I can get stuck here—raging against the dark, trying to figure out the win, the reason, the why. And then I remember: The enemy wants separation and death. That's it. It's not more complicated than that.

Again, this is a good time to remind ourselves that we are not fighting against flesh and blood but that the costs and consequences of evil are felt in real bodies and manifest themselves right here and right now. True, biblical spirituality is rooted in flesh and blood, in bodies and earth, dirt and relationships. This is why the Incarnation is the pivotal prototype of God's power at work in this world—through presence and embodied faith, through connection and real relationships, through healing and wholeness, through food and parties, through death and suffering, through resurrection and hope. All done right here in bodily form.

We connect and move toward life. That's what we *do*. How we do this takes on thousands of different forms. Sometimes it's a simple move toward making genuine connections and relationships with people from different backgrounds, ethnicities, religions, or sexual orientations. We move in the opposite spirit of the enemy who would seek to disconnect us and then destroy us. We fight for honest and genuine relationships—for real connection. We resist the Netflix binge and volunteer instead. We host a game night at our home to include our friends who don't have the money to go out for dinner. We move to a neighborhood to be present and open in the opposite direction of "upward mobility." We financially support good people doing good work in ways we can't—artists, justice workers, NGOs, social entrepreneurs, next-gen leaders . . . the options are endless and awesome. We use our homes as sanctuaries. We welcome refugees. We foster kids.

Recently, I've been asking people with backyards to open them for affordable housing and peaceful hospitality to people struggling with the housing crisis.[10] It turns out people struggling with houselessness don't just need houses—they need homes, community, connection. And guess what? It turns out people living the "suburban dream" of Western culture don't just need homes either; they also need community and connection. We need each other. And this is the most incredible truth of fighting against evil with the light, love, and life of Jesus. It liberates us all together. We are connected in suffering, and we are connected in resurrection. We only truly receive life abundant together.

And this is another manifestation of God's power in real life—relationships. Genuine connection. For far too long, we have thought theology, ideas, principles, or systems could right wrongs and usher in God's Kingdom—but they will not. This is the very kind of thinking that created residential schools in Canada and the USA[11]—*Let's take those "poor, pagan Indians" without the light of God and educate them in the "ways of God."* A systemic answer to a theological problem? Or a perpetuation of evil, a separation from, a killing, a stealing, and then death and destruction? God save us from ideological and systemic ideals, from principles to work with instead of people to love. God's power is manifested in people. And people express this power through connection and life.

So, maybe the best question is not what *can* we do but what *will* we do. What will we do as followers of Jesus, who told us that what we did to the "least of these" we did to him (Matthew 25:40)? What will we do when we discover there is a sacred calling to authentic faith in the most mundane and seemingly small acts of kindness and love toward others? What will we do when we grasp our interconnected destinies? I pray we will walk in the light, live in love, and move toward each other. This is our best hope for real change, inside and out.

9

A PEOPLE OF (GLAD) HOPE

Aubrey Sampson

THOUGH I'VE MOVED AROUND MOST OF MY LIFE, my roots were first planted in the red dirt and bluebonnets of Texas. To say "I was born in Texas" is also to say that I was born into a football family. I come from a long line of legendary (if only in their own minds) football players and fans. When I first began dating my now-husband Kevin, a guy from Chicago, the first thing my dad asked was whether he played football. He did; Dad approved and spread the word, "Y'all, he's from above the Mason-Dixon Line, but he plays football. So, it'll be okay."

Just before I started middle school, we moved to Oklahoma. My father, who had once played football for

Texas Tech, nearly dismantled the entire family system when he declared that from now on we would be University of Oklahoma football fans. He bought plastic travel coffee mugs, T-shirts, and a front-door flag to prove it, *Boomer Sooner*. It was then that I learned that while blood may be thicker than water, that is decidedly untrue when said water is the Red River—the natural, territorial boundary line between Texas and Oklahoma. My father had placed a stake in the river, and we were officially the rivals of my Texas family members. A fun and beloved rivalry, to be sure, but a dividing line now existed, nonetheless. It was us versus them.

Being the individualist that I am, I once tried to convince my family to start a Sunday-afternoon movie tradition rather than watching football. My mom simply said, "Aubrey, we can find any other time for a movie, but Sunday football is something we do together. This is community. This is a family thing."

The biblical writer Luke tells his readers a true story about Jesus at another type of community and family gathering, a dinner party. Jesus was invited to a prominent Pharisee's home, and after sitting back to watch the dinner party guests doggedly fight over the best seats at the table, Jesus reprimanded them. But he didn't stop there. Jesus turned his attention to the host and spoke pointedly:

> "When you give a luncheon or dinner, do not invite your friends, your brothers or sisters, your relatives, or your rich neighbors; if you do, they may invite

you back and so you will be repaid. But when you give a banquet, invite the poor, the crippled, the lame, the blind, and you will be blessed. Although they cannot repay you, you will be repaid at the resurrection of the righteous."

LUKE 14:12-14

Jesus was saying to this host and to the entire dinner party, "Look, you invited the wrong people to this meal. You invited those who will or at least *have the ability to* pay you back, those you can get something from. But if you wanted to have the kind of party that God blesses, you should have gone out into the streets and invited the people who are unable to give you anything in return. You should have invited the wounded, the worried, the weary, the weak, the war-torn. You and these dinner guests—your community here—should have been more concerned with bringing hope to your neighbors, inviting them to your dinners and gatherings and tables, rather than striving to take the good seats at this one."

In other words, we ought to be in the habit of offering seats of honor to those who are typically treated with dishonor—and furthermore, *this is something we do together. This is community. This is a family thing.*

Yet in a culture that celebrates rivalry, Jesus' word is as difficult for us as it was for his dinner host and guests. Whether it is out of good-natured sports fandom or because of more sinister motives, humanity loves to draw dividing lines—even when we are called by Jesus himself to erase them.

So how do we truly live out Jesus' mandate to invite in "the other," when we'd rather distance ourselves from them? When we'd rather keep the good seats for ourselves? When we'd rather cling to our boundary lines and divisions? And perhaps most importantly, how do we begin to do that *together*?

A People of Glad Hope

One of the many reasons my family loves football is because at the start of each new season, *hope springs eternal.*[1] The slate is clean. This could be *the* year our team finally succeeds. Each fall, football fans are filled with the hope, joy, and delight of what could be.

Interestingly, the late theologian Marva Dawn argued that the church ought to be marked by and recognized for something similar—its "hilarity," a Greek word from Romans 12:8, *hilarotēs*, meaning cheerfulness or *glad hope.*[2]

Similarly, theology professor Beth Felker Jones says this of the church: "The church of Jesus Christ is *this* joyous community: the community that rejoices in God's gracious salvation. The church is the community that opens up, through that grace, to proclaim Christ's peace to those 'who were far off' and to 'those who were near' (Eph. 2:17)."[3] We are a community marked by joy in God's gracious salvation.

In other words, the church—the expression of the triune God's multifaceted glory, joy, love, power, and wisdom on display for all to see, is also the redeemed family of God— a diverse, global, historic family—who were once separated from God and from one another but because of Jesus' work on the cross and resurrection are now united in belonging to him. And as God's redeemed family, we have been empowered by the Spirit to display and declare God's *glad gospel hope* wherever we have been planted.

God's Dream for the World

Any robust theology of *glad gospel hope* centers itself in God's overarching story, which is this: Since the beginning of time, God has had a dream for the world. God's dream is about overcoming evil and chaos, making for himself a people, and giving those people wholeness, flourishing, and a new identity in him.

In Genesis 1 and 2, we are told of God's power over the formlessness of the world and of the Spirit's hovering over the chaotic waters. Into that formless, chaotic void, God speaks—bringing life, order, and beauty. Then, God creates Adam and Eve in his image and places them in a *locale*, a garden, which they are invited to tend and cultivate.

Of course, we know that the shadow of sin creeps in, threatening to destroy God's dream. But God's dream is unstoppable; it culminates in the life, baptism, ministry, love, sacrifice, resurrection, and future return of Jesus Christ.

In Jesus, the dream that God started in Genesis 1 and continued throughout all of biblical history, across time and space, *the dream of overcoming evil forever, making for himself a people, and bringing new creation and garden-like flourishing to all*, is brought about. And as the redeemed family of God, united in our union with and under Jesus, we are the expression of that dream today.

The church is invited to respond to, participate in, and invite others into God's dream. We are called to declare and display, pronounce and perform, show and tell the message of God's dream—the message of glad gospel hope—to the communities and people where God has placed us. Here it bears repeating: *This is something we do together. This is community. This is a family thing.*

A Family on Mission

As the people of glad gospel hope in Christ, the church is given both a cultural mandate and a great commission. Like Adam and Eve before us, we are here to help cultivate our corners of the world into garden-like places so that humanity can thrive and multiply. The prophet Jeremiah similarly calls God's redeemed people to "build houses and settle down; plant gardens and eat what they produce. Marry and have sons and daughters. . . . Increase in number there; do not decrease. Also, seek the peace and prosperity of the city to which I have carried you into exile. Pray to the LORD for it, because if it prospers, you too will prosper" (Jeremiah 29:4-7). This is our cultural mandate too.

And alongside the early disciples of Jesus, we also have a great commission—go and make disciples, baptizing them in the name of the Father, Son, and Spirit (Matthew 28:19-20). It's worth noting that we also have a great commandment— to love God and love our neighbors—which encompasses both our mandate and our commission (Matthew 22:36-40).

In other words, God's glad-hope people have been sent

on God's glad-hope mission. Our cultural mandate and our great commission together make our *missio Dei*, or the mission of God for the people of God.

Yet in some of our more individualistic cultures, we have reduced the *missio Dei* to mean that we are called to be *individuals* of glad gospel hope. So *I* deliver a meal to a new mom, or *I* help a neighbor buy some groceries for the month. *I* mow someone's lawn when they are recovering from surgery, or *I* pay for someone's coffee in the drive-thru line behind me. These "I" acts are wildly important acts of compassion in this hurting world. But they do not tell the whole story of glad gospel hope.

As an aside, this individualistic mindset can swing in the opposite direction. We might grow afraid of certain types of individual acts of compassion. We do not want our loved ones to put themselves in harm's way, even if it would minister glad hope to someone in need. So we say things like "I don't want my wife picking up that unhoused man / drunk guy / prostitute on the highway. That will put her in danger." Then, because we struggle to move beyond an individualized response to those in need, we become paralyzed in our fear and do nothing.

To be sure, our individual acts of compassion matter, *and* our fears for our loved ones are legitimate. Still, the earliest disciples and apostles would have been baffled by our individualist interpretations of our cultural mandate and commission. "Of course you wouldn't send your wife to pick up the displaced person alone. We do that as a Christian community. And sure, you can pay for someone's coffee, but what if the church in your neighborhood pooled its resources and bought coffee for everyone in need? Or better yet, what if you all bought a coffee shop, created new jobs, dedicated a new space for community gatherings, and helped the whole neighborhood flourish? Or what if your entire small group frequented a local coffee shop, boosting the economy and building loving, mutually beneficial relationships with the employees and regulars?"

What I mean is, the earliest disciples might look at us and say, "Yes! Your individual acts of compassion are Christlike, but what if you're thinking too small?"

If indeed the church is a redeemed family marked by glad gospel hope, then we ought to move beyond our myopic individual expressions and think bigger, as a people.

Again, *this is something we do together. This is community. This is a family thing.*

Glad Hope Outside the Margins

Remember Luke's story of Jesus at the Pharisee's dinner party? Think about who Jesus was calling the dinner guests to minister to—those outside of their normal boundaries. The Pharisees were known for putting up dividing walls, keeping themselves separate from "the unholy" in order to protect their own holiness. But Jesus, the only truly holy one among us, was unafraid to cross those boundaries. With this posture, Jesus was continuing what his Father before him had been doing all along.

Consider Hagar from Genesis 16 and 21. Hagar's story is often sadly "reduced to a strategic mistake in the life of Abraham and Sarah, with Hagar's son Ishmael becoming a false answer to God's covenant promise to Abraham."[4]

A more careful reading of Hagar's story reveals God's heart for the enslaved, the woman, and the foreigner.[5] Hagar's story is about God's compassionate heart *as well as* God's desire to display his sovereignty and goodness beyond the boundaries of Israel. While Hagar's tale could be interpreted as a threat to God's promises to Abraham, Hagar actually shows us something else—an expansion in God's mission beyond the boundaries. In fact, it is through *Hagar's* perspective, not Abraham's or Sarah's, that the mission of God expands to the nations, revealing that God actively engages with all nations and all communities. As Hagar and Ishmael's story unfolds, we find that many nations will have the opportunity to know Hagar's "God who sees" (Genesis 16:13).[6]

In other words, where we have placed dividing lines, God crosses them. God crosses human cultures, human barriers, and human hearts to expand his mission, that dream of old—*God's dream of overcoming evil forever, making for himself a people, and bringing new creation and garden-like flourishing to all through his Son, Jesus.*

When we begin to recognize that pharisaical *holier-than-thou* tendency within us—it is an invitation to ask God to regospel *us.* We must invite the Spirit of God to remind us how great a salvation we have received in Jesus—who, while we were still sinners, still unwelcome, still with no seat at the table, died for us. God did not separate himself from us when we were covered in our sin and shame but drew near and invited us in.

In response to God's great love for us, how might the entire church, God's people of glad gospel hope, begin to do the same for others?

Communities of Hope Bringers

If we are here as the expression of God's dream for the world, then what does it look like for us, as communities of Christ followers, to meet the needs of those in our midst? We get a clue from the apostles Peter and John in Acts 3:

> One day Peter and John were going up to the temple at the time of prayer—at three in the afternoon. Now a man who was lame from birth was being carried to the temple gate called Beautiful, where he was put every day to beg from those going into the temple courts. When he saw Peter and John about to enter, he asked them for money. *Peter looked straight at him, as did John.* Then Peter said, "Look at us!" So the man gave them his attention, expecting to get something from them.
>
> Then Peter said, "Silver or gold I do not have, but what I do have I give you. In the name of Jesus Christ of Nazareth, walk." Taking him by the right hand, he helped him up, and instantly the man's feet and ankles became strong. He jumped to his feet and began to

walk. Then he went with them into the temple courts, walking and jumping, and praising God.

ACTS 3:1-8, EMPHASIS ADDED

This sick man experienced the holistic love of Jesus, as Peter and John *together*, in the midst of the onlooking community, fulfilled the cultural mandate, the great commission, and the great commandment—declaring and displaying a glad gospel hope that included

- *Dignity.* This was a man outside of the boundaries of his day, considered unclean and dishonored in Jewish culture. But the disciples looked and truly *saw*, as God saw Hagar. They dignified him as the image bearer he was.

- *Wholeness.* The disciples healed this man physically. But they also took the time to lift him up, and they saw his emotions explode with delight! This man also experienced spiritual healing, knowing that Jesus was the one who set him free from the chaos that had controlled his body for his entire life.

- *Restoration.* This man was able to move toward community and worship with others. This was a new day for him, where he experienced belonging and family.

- *Refreshment.* He was free from suffering, finally able to experience shalom and rest.

- *Repentance.* After this healing, Peter proclaimed a message of repentance to the healed man and the shocked onlookers.

As Christian communities situated in our current time and place, we have tended to focus *solely* on that last part—repentance. But the early church fathers and mothers assumed that we would always be operating with a communal expression of compassionate evangelism, including a holistic gospel message.

What if church communities all around the world began thinking biblically about our evangelism efforts? How might we proclaim a gospel of dignity, wholeness, restoration, refreshment, and repentance outside our typical boundaries?

This might mean an entire church bringing its resources together to meet the needs of a local refugee family, welcoming them into the fold. This could look like a missional community using its networks, connections, and finances to help launch a single mom into a life of well-stewarded fiscal responsibility for her future and for her kids' future. This might mean a small group of Christians walking alongside an unhoused man. It might mean several churches pooling their funds to support a dying local neighborhood business. It could mean gathering around a local sex-trafficking victim to be her friend and help her consider rehabilitation. It could mean gathering with other Christians for a peaceful protest or lament protest when an injustice has occurred in the neighborhood or city.

At our little multiethnic church plant in West Chicago, Illinois, we have tried to do a few things to bring glad gospel hope and fulfill the *missio Dei* in our corner of the world. We have combined our resources to give to a local Christian soccer ministry to offer sports ministry to those who might not otherwise be able to afford it. We have banded together in small groups to become Friendship Partners through World Relief, walking alongside several refugee families. (As a result of this mutuality-based friendship, we have seen many refugees come to Christ and get baptized.)

We partnered with other churches to offer food pantries in the middle of the COVID-19 pandemic. We helped support a local coffee shop when it was struggling, and a local *paletería* (ice-cream shop) as well. We have gathered for "dinner, documentary, and discussion nights" to talk about racial injustice. We have given rugs, books, and other supplies to our under-resourced local schools, many of which our kids attend.

None of this, we pray, has been done with a "savior" complex but all of it has been done with an eye toward the risen Savior. All of it has been done with God's deep love. We want to be a church known for its glad gospel hope. We want our neighbors to experience true flourishing, in Jesus' name.

Once, a teacher in our local community died unexpectedly, and our church was asked to hold and lead a school funeral service for her. *Why us?* Because the school did not know any other church community who would be willing to enter the needs of the school. While there are a lot of church leaders in our town who would have taken this on, it was encouraging to us that our neighborhood saw Renewal Church as a resource *for them*.

Sometimes in our desire to *change the world*, we miss out on the fact that being good neighbors with the gospel in our hands is all we ever really need to be. Silver or gold we may not have, but what we do have, we are invited to give—the name and love of Jesus—to the hurting people around us.

Still, can I be honest about something? Fulfilling our communal mandate and commission comes at a cost, and as you likely know, it will come at a cost for your community, your church. We have been insulted by other local evangelical churches. We've been called "woke, progressive, social-justice warriors."

So consider this your fair warning: When your church family comes together in catholicity with other churches, or in what Alan Hirsch calls *communitas* (organic community on mission),[7] to become bringers of glad gospel hope in Jesus, Satan will have a field day. Dividing walls will go up.

Still, that does not change your mission. The redeemed family of God, on the mission of God, are hope bringers.

Children of Light

In his letter to the Ephesian church, the apostle Paul reminds the Christian community situated in Ephesus to "live as children of light" (Ephesians 5:8). It is no accident that Paul tells them and by extension, *us*, to live as the plural, *children*. Paul knows that the church will display greater gospel effectiveness, greater love, greater glad hope when we shine brightly in our identity *together* as God's redeemed family.

Speaking of family, one of the biggest football fans in my own clan was my cousin Cameron, a ride-or-die University of Texas Longhorns fan. Cameron and my dad had a massive rivalry, with Dad egging Cam on for his love of UT; Cam doing the same for my dad's traitorous affection for Oklahoma football.

One devastating day in 2015, Cameron stepped out onto a snow cornice in Crater Lake National Park, Oregon, and plummeted to his death. We held Cameron's funeral at an airplane hangar in Nashville, at the airport where Cameron worked as a pilot. My dad said a few words at the service, then ended his speech by pulling out a Longhorns hat, donning it in Cameron's honor. We all sobbed. The rivalry was over. *This was a family thing.*

When the sun went down that evening, we launched more than a dozen floating paper lanterns into the Nashville night sky and watched as they gently made their journeys onward, little flames of glad hope lighting up the dense darkness of our grief.

A few days before the funeral, my family had had a conversation about the floating lanterns. *Would we all step outside the airport hangar and watch my aunt, Cameron's mom, launch a single floating lantern?* Maybe. That would have been beautiful, we agreed. In many ways, that single act would have been enough to say something, to mean something, to honor Cameron and our family's grief. But something about that did not feel right. It felt too small, somehow. We kept brain-storming and came to another conclusion.

As a prophetic act, as a declaration of our longing, as a sign of life in the face of this horrendous tragedy, we decided to light up the sky, not with a solitary lantern but with a community of lights.

What no one said until later was that we all silently prayed that somebody across the city—somebody who might be wounded, worried, weary, weak, or war-torn in their own way, someone on the outside of the "seat of honor" in their community—would look up. We prayed that *that* somebody would see our flotilla of lanterns alighting the sky. And we prayed that for one moment that hurting soul might have their wonder reignited . . . might have their imagination turned on . . . might have their own darkness lit up with glad hope.

The call to live as a church marked by glad gospel hope—well, it isn't cute or precious. Our cities, our communities, our corners of the world are in pain; the darkness is encroaching. This communal mandate and communal commission to live as children of light, as the redeemed people of God on the mission of God, is a call to cross boundaries and go toe-to-toe with the darkness—in and through and for the great name of Jesus.

This is what we do. This is community. This is a family thing.

10

GOD WILL WIPE EVERY TEAR FROM THEIR EYES

Christiana Rice

HE LEFT A MESS OF TRASH on the edge of our neighborhood park, including the ashy remnants of a mini bonfire. Chunks of Styrofoam were sprinkled in the bushes, food containers had been tossed around, and a well-worn jacket hung on a branch nearby. I had greeted the man for several days while he camped out at the park. He was an older gentleman with bright eyes who spent his time alone, often talking to himself, his body weathered by a complex story that wrinkled his skin, muddled his mind, and clouded his disposition. The man was kind, though, and sometimes he handed me bags of bottles and cans, suggesting I go make some money at a local recycling center.

Every Wednesday, a small group of my neighbors gather to clean up trash at this park. We meet on the corner of A and Twenty-Fifth Streets, wearing gloves and carrying reusable containers as we hunt for trash with reverence, acknowledging that some of our outdoor neighbors consider this park their home. Yet no matter how much trash we clear, there's always more. Shards of glass like confetti in the grass, graffiti sprayed on trees, open needles, saucy magazines, and the daily littering of fast-food containers and unopened mini packets of condiments. Trash is everywhere and everyday, a small symbol of an insufferable dilemma of our society and the environment. God help us.

Like life itself, this park is both beautiful and broken. We wonder if it's worth contending for it, protecting it, and working for justice when the everyday suffering of our world seems unremitting. The land suffers, the creatures suffer, the minds and bodies of our neighbors suffer, and we forget our sacred interrelatedness that means it all belongs together. Will this suffering ever end? Why bother picking up trash when the world will be trashed again tomorrow? Why bother?

Yet there is an undercurrent of truth that flows deeper than the ground we walk on. The current of God's redemption upholds us, knits us back together, and nurtures us, reminding us that all suffering is indeed temporal and the possibilities of new life are bubbling just beneath the surface, ready to push through and spring over. Waters of new life!

So how do we live with suffering while contending for this hopeful reality of new life, remembering that Christ is with us in the pain and in the birthing? "In this world you will have trouble," Jesus said as he walked his neighborhood and traveled through surrounding towns, his feet on the ground, "But take heart! I have overcome the world" (John 16:33). Christ's overcoming presence is for the now *and* the not yet. God knows about the trash; God sees every tear; God welcomes every groan and labors for the birth of the new creation as we wait and care and contend. This is the Christian decree: that all will be made new. A decree worth hoping for, living for, fighting for, and for some of us, it's worth picking up trash for.

The Ashes of Our Lives

The Christian story and church calendar have much to say about the cyclical nature of suffering marbled with a curious hope of a mysterious and liberative future. Ash Wednesday is one of those mile markers on the spiritual journey that invites Christ followers to remember our mortality, repent of the ways we diverge from God's path of love, and mourn over the suffering of our world. As many of us have experienced, traditionally a priest or pastor presses their finger into a dish of ashes and makes an impression of a cross on one's forehead. This tangible symbol of ashes and the sign of the cross are significant, most often related to the experience of personal and collective suffering and lament.

This year on Ash Wednesday, I paused at the remains of a mini bonfire that my outdoor neighbor had left behind in our park. I impulsively dipped my finger in the ashes, smearing it on my forehead in the sign of a cross saying, "I take *these* ashes—the ashes of my neighbor and of my neighborhood, of all who experience mental illness, the ashes of a fractured social system, the ashes of a humiliated habitat—the ashes of suffering." Then I scooped up a handful of ashes and brought them home to display on our counter in the bed of a large shell we found at a San Diego beach. The ashes and shell stayed visible though the season of Lent— a memento of suffering and hope.

Ashes have been a potent element for our community lately. On March 19, 2021, I watched and wailed as a funeral-home transporter came to pick up the breathless body of my neighbor, best friend, and beloved sister-in-law, Rebecca, who died too soon of metastasized breast cancer. They wrapped her in a green velvet cloth and strapped her to a wooden gurney, carrying her body from her enchanting little bedroom to an unmarked white van with no side windows. Days later, the mortician placed a bag of ashes in my arms, and I almost collapsed under the weight of them, the weight of grief. Her ashes were heavier than I had imagined. As Scripture says, "Dust you are and to dust you will return" (Genesis 3:19). What remained of Rebecca's beautiful body was three pounds of dust, and I clutched it to my chest as if I'd discovered gold.

We hosted her memorial service in a neighborhood backyard and then walked to our park for a community-wide reception, celebrating a life that was but is no more. What a strange dichotomy, really. Not unlike the night we gathered at my house to shave Rebecca's head after her first couple of rounds of chemotherapy. We gathered in suffering and courageous hope. Pink war paint on our faces, we each took turns shaving off strips of her hair, watching it fall to the ground like the clippings of rose buds. Then we blasted India.Arie's "I Am Not My Hair."[1] We were dancing on injustice, an audacious dichotomy of suffering and hope that carried us through what became a four-year journey with terminal cancer.

This park has been a meeting point for significant and simple moments of life. Like when I held Rebecca in a tight embrace, sitting on a bench, my hand on her bald head as she emerged from yet another week of chemo recovery, trying to catch her breath and hold on to the fringes of faith. Or when I sat face-to-face with a beloved community mate, listening and sharing as we plowed through misunderstanding to uncover a path of peace. Or hosting a socially distanced benefit concert at the park just after the senseless murder of George Floyd in Minneapolis, Minnesota. At this park we've wept and belly laughed, conveyed deep love, and sat for hours with wearying sorrow. We've marked birthdays and milestones, transitions and competitions. We've watched the sunset countless times, and sometimes we just lay in the grass and stare at the sky, breathing deep with gratitude. Our park is part of our parish where we meet God and one another through the valleys and peaks of life, through suffering and hope.

What if Christians were known as those who tenderly hold the ashes of the world, clutching them to our chest like gold? How do we become hosts of celebration and suffering, honoring spaces and places with our attentive presence? The very essence of our faith is founded on a God who suffers for us and alongside us. Perhaps our greatest solidarity with one another and with the most vulnerable comes from the most particular suffering and joy of our everyday lives in our everyday places, like our living rooms, cafés, sidewalks, and parks. And perhaps our deepest connection with God is in divine comfort during our darkest, ashiest of hours.

Were You There?

I grew up in a missionary family in the city of Tokyo, Japan. After four years of education in the Japanese school system, I transferred to Christian Academy in Japan, an international school taught in English, originally founded as a school for missionary kids. Though my neighbors were Japanese and I had Japanese friends, I was raised in a "missionary community" where many of my school and church peers were from all over the world, their families immersed in ministry contexts all over the city. The tradition of Christianity was baked into the life of our family, not as a religious obligation but as a vocational assignment—I was taught to see my life pursuit as central to the mission of God: to love people and help them know the love of God through Jesus their Savior. As for suffering, we knew God was with us to comfort us but ultimately that our hope was founded on a theology of salvation that would one day set us free from pain as we depart this earth and dance our way through the pearly gates of heaven.

Singing the "hymns of old" was a regular pastime for our family that helped us hold on to this hope of our eternal home in heaven. We sang hymns and choruses at gatherings big and small, in both Japanese and English; we sang them at church services or holiday events with friends who became like extended family. Worshiping God through music and connecting to the songs of our Christian history was a lifeline for the adults in my life, and I grew to love the practice of it.

"Were You There" is a hymn typically referencing Good Friday, when we remember the torturous crucifixion of Jesus on the cross. We sang this song throughout the year, yet I was oblivious to its original intent and passion. Well into my adulthood I discovered that "Were You There" is an African American spiritual, born out of the collective African American slave experience, directly connecting the crucifixion of Jesus to the public, torturous lynching of Black slaves. This is not just a song of repentance but a song of solidarity, of lament, of honest grief and holy empathy.

Were you there when they crucified my Lord? . . .
Were you there when they nailed him to the tree? . . .
Were you there when they laid him in the tomb? . . .
Were you there when God raised him from the tomb?
Oh, sometimes it causes me to tremble, tremble, tremble.
Were you there when God raised him from the tomb?[2]

In my youth, I believed in a particular theology that said our sin and sinfulness is what lifted Jesus onto that cross; it was our fault that he had to die, and we should tremble at the thought. It's also a theology that equates our moral purity and even our eternal salvation with the acceptance of this sacrifice that Jesus willingly made for us.

I remember performing a solo in church called "Feel the Nails," by Ray Boltz. The lyrics ask, "Does he still feel the nails every time I fail?"[3] Toward the end of the song, the cassette-tape background track had the harsh pounding noise of a hammer crashing onto a nail, reinforcing how painful it must have been to have a nail hammered into your wrist the way Jesus had to endure, for us! These words and sounds were meant to fortify both our Christian conviction and holy guilt, intended to lead to a passionate repentance. *It was me who did this! And oh, God, I'm so sorry that I'm not capable of being any better.*

I've come to learn that the torture and death and resurrection of Jesus is much more revolutionary than a theory of replacement for punishment. The suffering of Jesus was for us and with us. As the African American slaves knew so well, there is a reciprocal solidarity between God and God's creation. God, were you there when they hung us on the tree? Were we there when you suffered and died on the cross? Were you there? Are you there? Do we remember? Do we trust that you are with us in our suffering? Do we hold hope for liberation, for the birth of the new creation, now and not yet?

The unresolved yet consoling questions posed in this hymn are invaluable for all who suffer. How do we bring the past to the present in such a way that we know God in our suffering and we trust that God knows us in the suffering of the world? In *The Cross and the Lynching Tree*, theologian James Cone notes that the cross is central to the African American experience. He says, "During my childhood . . . there were more songs, sermons, prayers, and testimonies about the cross than any other theme. The cross was the foundation on which [my congregation's] faith was built. In the mystery of God's revelation, Black Christians believed that just knowing that Jesus went through an experience of suffering in a manner similar to theirs gave them faith that God was with them, even in suffering on lynching trees, just as God was present with Jesus in suffering on the cross."[4] Another profound perspective here. Were you there, God, when they hung Jesus on the cross? What an honest question that everyone is bound to ask in our hour of greatest sorrow and need: *God, are you even there?* Questions like these do not diminish the Resurrection; they sustain us in the waiting. God is there, God is here, God is with us, just as God was with Jesus on the cross.

Pack Your Tambourine

Miriam, the sister of Moses, is a character in the biblical narrative who embodied a fierce and persistent hope in God amid her own suffering and the suffering of her people. She was imperfect, like the rest of us, but a valiant example of one who believed and trusted in a God of deliverance. In Exodus 2, we read of Miriam, a sister who courageously saves her baby brother from impending genocide. Then in

Exodus 15, Miriam is named as a prophet who leads the Hebrew women to sing and dance and play drums, publicly partying after they cross the Red Sea to safety.

What I want to highlight here is how Miriam lived a life prepared for deliverance. Miriam cared, contended, and sometimes complained as her people remained enslaved and her dreams of deliverance felt like a distant mist. Yet Miriam packed her tambourine. The very act of keeping the tambourine on hand was a symbol of her faith, holding hope that deliverance would come and she'd soon be celebrating the redemption of God for her people. She heard from God and she trusted that the promises of God's deliverance would come true, so she packed her instrument of victory, of jubilee, of joy! Scripture calls Miriam a prophet (Exodus 15:20), the first woman in the Bible to be credited with prophetic contribution. She leads the women in singing and dancing, playing her tambourine as a declarative instrument of hope.

A few years ago, our neighborhood church community mourned over the deportation of an undocumented immigrant neighbor. Her story was complex, but after thirty years of living in the US, she was deported and was unable to return to her home and her family. As we prayed together, we remembered the thousands of refugees and asylum seekers, traveling miles and miles by foot to escape violence and corruption. Many of these migrant caravans set up camp communities at the edge of the US-Mexico border, longing for a miracle of God to part the way for them. How do you pray for something that seems so impossible? We have Mexican national friends who transformed church buildings into shelters and sought to strengthen the network of care in Tijuana. We brought truckloads of donations, and we supported with whatever resources we had to give. Still, displaced and dispossessed people groups continue to be a global crisis. Can they pack their tambourines in the desert, where they keep walking and hoping? God, are you there?

I'm not sure I have any answers for how to survive the sheer reality of suffering in this world. Many have suffered far more than I will ever understand. Yet with the most broken as our guides, I do believe we can all keep moving forward, keep dancing and linking arms with the comforting and guiding presence of God, who will never leave us. We can work for the peace and justice of Jesus as a vocational assignment of God, wherever God has placed us. We can pack our tambourines and keep walking toward collective deliverance.

Keep Moving

In his address at Spelman College on April 10, 1960, Dr. Martin Luther King Jr. urged the audience to never stop working for peace and liberation, saying, "If you can't fly, run; if you can't run, walk; if you can't walk, crawl; but by all means keep moving."[5] This quote has animated thousands of activists, artists, peacemakers, and practitioners all over the world for over sixty years. Dr. King knew that to hold hope means we keep moving toward the dream of God, and we keep moving together. Perhaps it is in this togetherness that we find the presence of the Holy Spirit and the hope to stay the course, even in our suffering.

Oppressed people model this: the enslaved, the impoverished, and the sick. My sister-in-law Rebecca modeled this kind of resilient hope more than anyone I've known. She walked through the valley of the shadow of death with her head held high, her emotions honest, and her eyes fixed on Jesus, the author and refiner of her faith (Hebrews 12:2). Rebecca kept moving, and she knew that the Spirit of God was with her every step of the way, even until her day of death. And now, on the other side, where she is no longer with us and we continue to walk in the valley of the shadow after death, we keep moving, God beside us, among us, within us.

As Jesus left the earth, he left us with this great gift of Holy Spirit presence. Even in a world of trouble, Jesus assured us, "You'll never be alone" (Matthew 28:20, author's paraphrase). We are accompanied by God, enveloped in the created world, woven together in the community of Christ followers called "the church," interdependent with our neighbors, and in this way, we come to know in our bodies the promise of God's deliverance in the now and for eternity.

Friends, God will wipe away every tear from our eyes (Revelation 21:4). So keep moving. Smear the ashes of your neighborhood on your forehead, dance on injustice, wear pink war paint on your cheeks, pack your tambourine, and be ready to start playing a beat of jubilee. Keep moving through the valley. God is with us, and we are never alone.

CONTINUING THE CONVERSATION

Questions for Reflection and Discussion

KINGDOM CONVERSATIONS RAISE THE STAKES as we allow God to bring his higher thoughts to bear on our limited vision and finite wisdom. We don't just interact thoughtfully; we do so prayerfully, subjecting ourselves to the sovereignty of a God who loves us and wants good for us and from us. And we do so both individually and collectively, not settling merely for personal reflection that deepens our private piety, or for dialogue that ends in chin-stroking self-congratulation. Rather, we engage in honest and humble conversation with God, with ourselves, and with others so that we can see where Jesus is leading us now to proclaim and demonstrate, near and far, that God is here, God is good, and God is for us. A Kingdom conversation has the potential, in small and big ways, to transform the world.

What follows are questions to prime the pump for these Kingdom conversations. Almost every question is designed to be considered from two perspectives: personally, for the purposes of private and public reflection and confession;

and corporately, in order to listen to and learn from other perspectives, to learn to love one another, and to seek God together as a faith community.

The questions are organized by chapter in case you wish to move slowly through the book together. If you wish to discuss the book as a whole in one conversation, it's best to review the questions ahead of time and focus together on the questions that help you move from curiosity to conviction, from head to heart to hands.

Introduction

- Why did you decide to read this book?

Chapter 1: Who Is My Neighbor?

- When you think of your "neighbors," who are the first people who come to mind? Where are they located? As you reflect a bit longer, who else does God bring to your mind?
- Who are the "Ruths" in your midst—the women and men society views as the least of these? Are you willing not just to notice them but to let them teach you?
- When have you observed glimpses of hope and joy amid dire, desperate circumstances, as the author did when she saw children's drawings at the migrant shelter?
- How will you invite "strangers" into your life in the next week, the next month, the next year?

Chapter 2: Created in His Image

- Prior to reading this chapter, how would you have described what makes someone "human," or the idea that human beings are created in God's image?
- How can you better show the people around you the value that God has created them with and treat them as true brothers and sisters? Think of a specific person.
- Do you view *yourself* as highly valuable?
- Take one day and during your interactions, pause to recognize that each person you talk to or pass by is created in the image of God. How does this change your perspective of them, your understanding of God, and your own heart?

Chapter 3: A History of Compassion

- Which story in this chapter moved you or spoke to you the most? Why?
- When are you most prone to trying to bring change by your own power, to "leapfrog the message of the gospel" and the power of God's love?
- How is God calling you to simple yet steadfast faithfulness? Do you believe that this faithfulness can bring about great change?
- Would you say you are currently abiding in God's vine and delighting in Christ?

- Take a moment to talk with God about what you feel are your inadequacies. Allow yourself to rest in Christ's strength and love.

Chapter 4: Do Not Withhold Good

- How has this chapter challenged or changed your understanding of biblical teaching about social justice?
- Where might you be ignoring obvious needs around you? Where might you be tolerating injustice or showing favoritism to people of status, wealth, and privilege? What will you do to change these tendencies?
- Ask God to help you to not withhold good: to give you the eyes to see the needs around you, a heart to be moved to compassion, and the courage to take action.

Chapter 5: The Comprehensive Gospel

- How would you describe the gospel? Who and what has shaped your understanding of it?
- What is your response to the author's assertion that the gospel doesn't only have a personal dimension (uniting individuals with God) but also has a social dimension (uniting us with one another)? Is this understanding challenging to you? Why or why not?
- Based on the author's definition, has your understanding of the gospel been a full gospel or a truncated, partial gospel? Where are there gaps in your

gospel or misalignment in what you preach versus how you live?

- How can you and those in your faith community become full gospelizers, on earth as it is in heaven?

Chapter 6: The Power of Proximity

- Whom in our society—and even, if you're honest, in your own life—do you tend to view as "unclean" or "less than"?
- As the author asks: In what ways have you turned away from people who are around you every day, causing them to be in a desperate situation where their only choice is to seek a miracle from Jesus?
- How and where can you come closer to those on the margins through proximity, interaction, and relationship instead of turning away or distancing yourself?
- How can you and your faith community work not only to meet needs but also to devise longer-term solutions for those who need help?

Chapter 7: A Call for a Multi-Ability Church

- Have you ever considered your theology about disability? How would you describe it before and after reading this chapter?
- How does the reality that Jesus Christ was *broken* affect your perspective on human brokenness, weakness, and disability?

- Are you clear about and confident in how you have been created, called, and commissioned? What are your unique contributions as a connected member of the body of Christ?
- What is your unique context, and how do you live out your calling in that context?
- How can your faith community better minister *from* the margins and not just *to* the margins—participating, cultivating, and activating to become a true multi-ability church?

Chapter 8: What Can We Do?

- When was the last time you lamented? Whom or what was your lament for? How did you express it?
- How has God broken your heart for the things that break his? Where do you still have calluses over your heart or soul?
- In what situations are you most prone to misidentify and fight against human enemies instead of against the powers of darkness?
- How do you typically think about power? Is it a power over or a power under? A power of conquest and control or one of liberation? A power of possession or one of partnership? How might you need to reframe your understanding of God's power?
- Where in your mind, heart, and actions do you need to replace lies with truth, fear with love, or separation and death with connection and life?

Chapter 9: A People of (Glad) Hope

- Would you describe your church as a people of hope, even of glad hope? Why or why not?
- How do you demonstrate glad hope to those around you? Is this mostly an individual effort? How can you do this in community with others?
- Who are the people outside your faith community's typical boundaries? How might you together proclaim a gospel of dignity, wholeness, restoration, or refreshment to those people?
- When are you most tempted to be a savior to others instead of pointing people to *the* Savior?

Chapter 10: God Will Wipe Every Tear from Their Eyes

- What is your default response when you see suffering around you or hear about it occurring elsewhere?
- What are the "ashes" of suffering you see around you, the things you can carry with you internally or externally to remind you to lament the pain and brokenness in our world?
- What can be your "tambourine," your symbol of faith that God can bring better things to come?
- What are the ways God is calling you to keep moving, to keep working for peace, justice, healing, and restoration?

NOTES

CHAPTER 1: WHO IS MY NEIGHBOR?

1. This is a term coined by Mother Teresa in her book *In the Heart of the World: Thoughts, Stories & Prayers* (Novato, CA: New World Library, 1997).
2. Name has been changed to protect identity.
3. Name has been changed to protect identity.
4. Emily Dickinson, "'Hope' is the Thing with Feathers" from *The Complete Poems of Emily Dickinson*, ed. Thomas H. Johnson (Boston: Bay Back Books, 1998), 254.
5. National Immigration Forum, "Explainer: The Migrant Protection Protocols," August 25, 2021, https://immigrationforum.org/article /explainer-the-migrant-protection-protocols.
6. Gregory Boyle, *Tattoos on the Heart: The Power of Boundless Compassion* (New York: Free Press, 2011), 75.

CHAPTER 2: CREATED IN HIS IMAGE

1. For a helpful discussion on these issues see John F. Kilner, *Dignity and Destiny: Humanity in the Image of God* (Cambridge, UK: Eerdmans, 2015), 17–37.
2. Philippians 2:9-11; Hebrews 1:3; James 1:17; Revelation 4:11.
3. Romans 8:15; 9:26; Galatians 3:26; Ephesians 1:5; 2:19; 1 John 3:2.
4. 2 Corinthians 4:16; 1 Thessalonians 5:23; Hebrews 4:12.
5. For just a few examples see Psalm 82:3; Zechariah 7:9-10; Matthew 19:21; Galatians 6:2.
6. Psalm 74:21; Proverbs 31:8-9; Isaiah 58:6-8; Luke 14:12-14; Galatians 2:10; James 1:27; 1 John 3:16-18.

CHAPTER 3: A HISTORY OF COMPASSION

1. See, for example, William Gibson, *Samuel Wesley and the Crisis of Tory Piety, 1685–1720* (Oxford: Oxford University Press, 2021), 2.
2. British Library, "Timelines: Gin Addiction, 1751," accessed August 10, 2022, https://www.bl.uk/learning/timeline/item105855.html.
3. John Pollock, *Wesley the Preacher* (Eastbourne, UK: Kingsway Publications, 2000), 50.
4. Pollock, *Wesley the Preacher*, 98.
5. James Kiefer, "John and Charles Wesley," satucket.com, accessed August 10, 2022, http://satucket.com/lectionary/Wesley.htm.
6. W. E. H. Lecky, *History of England in the Eighteenth Century*, vol. 2 (London: Longmans, Green & Co., 1879), 558.
7. J. H. Plumb, *England in the Eighteenth Century* (Baltimore: Penguin Books, 1964), 93–94.
8. From Matthew 25:35, KJV. John Stott, *The Incomparable Christ* (Downers Grove, IL: IVP Books, 2001), 170.
9. William Hague, *William Wilberforce: The Life of the Great Anti-Slave Trade Campaigner* (Orlando: Harcourt, 2007), 119.
10. John Newton, "Thoughts upon the African Slave Trade," *Works of John Newton*, vol. 4 (Edinburgh: Banner of Truth, 2015), 694.
11. John Newton, "Memoirs of the Rev. John Newton," *Works of John Newton*, vol. 1 (Edinburgh: Banner of Truth, 2015), xxxvi.
12. John Newton, "Amazing Grace," 1779. Public domain.
13. Robert Isaac Wilberforce and Samuel Wilberforce, *The Life of William Wilberforce*, vol. 3, abridged from the London ed. by Caspar Morris (Philadelphia: Perkins, 1839), 46.
14. UK Wells, "John Newton (1725–1807)," accessed August 12, 2022, https://ukwells.org/revivalists/john-newton#.
15. Robert Isaac Wilberforce and Samuel Wilberforce, *The Life of William Wilberforce*, vol. 1, 2nd ed. (London: Murray, 1839), 149.
16. Britannica, "Slavery Abolition Act: United Kingdom (1833)," accessed August 10, 2022, https://www.britannica.com/topic/Slavery-Abolition-Act.
17. Olaudah Equiano, *The Interesting Narrative and Other Writings*, rev. ed. (New York: Penguin Books, 2003), 47.
18. Equiano, *Interesting Narrative and Other Writings*, 189–90.
19. National Justice Museum, "The 'Bloody Code'?" July 29, 2019, https://nationaljusticemuseum.co.uk/museum/news/what-was-the-bloody-code.
20. Peter King and Richard Ward, "Rethinking the Bloody Code in Eighteenth-Century Britain: Capital Punishment at the Centre and

on the Periphery," *Past & Present* 228, no. 1 (August 2015): 159–205, https://doi.org/10.1093/pastj/gtv026.

21. Newgate Prison Death Row Education Society, "The West View of Newgate Prison," accessed August 10, 2022, websites.umich.edu/~ece /student_projects/bonifield/newgatepic.html.

22. UK Wells, "Elizabeth Fry (1780–1845): Quaker Minister and Reformer," accessed August 10, 2022, https://ukwells.org/revivalists /elizabeth-fry.

23. As quoted in E. R. Pitman, *Elizabeth Fry*, Eminent Women series, ed. John H. Ingram (London: W. H. Allen & Co., 1884), 126.

24. This was fabricated but is in the style of many of the people we've studied in this chapter. For example, William Wilberforce wrote: "Alas. Alas! How little have all my Resolutions been remember'd during the last week, & how like has it gone on to the preceding," "Blessed be God for Sunday. Scott, an excellent sermon," and "By Grace we are saved—God of his great Mercy, even when we were dead in Sins, hath quicken'd us together with Christ etc. This only is my Hope!" from *William Wilberforce, His Unpublished Spiritual Journals*, ed. Michael D. McMullen (Fearn, Ross-shire, Great Britain: Christian Focus, 2021), 106, 112, 121.

CHAPTER 4: DO NOT WITHHOLD GOOD

1. See Judith McCartney and Colin McCartney, *What Does Justice Look Like and Why Does God Care about It?* The Jesus Way: Small Books of Radical Faith (Harrisonburg, VA: Herald Press, 2020), 13–17.

2. Bruce V. Malchow, *Social Justice in the Hebrew Bible: What Is New and What Is Old* (Collegeville, MN: Liturgical Press, 1996), 26–27.

3. Leslie J. Hoppe, *There Shall Be No Poor among You: Poverty in the Bible* (Nashville: Abingdon Press, 2004), 25.

4. Moshe Weinfeld, *Social Justice in Ancient Israel and in the Ancient Near East* (Minneapolis: Fortress Press, 1995), 18. Emphasis original.

5. Weinfeld, *Social Justice in Ancient Israel*, 18. See also Malchow, *Social Justice*, 63–75, for a discussion of social justice in Israel's Wisdom Literature.

6. Weinfeld, *Social Justice in Ancient Israel*, 19, refers to Matthew as a Gospel "in which the tradition drew upon Jewish norms." Matthew 25, of course, is well-known in many Christian circles as a passage that admonishes social justice in the form of providing food, clothing, and care for the incarcerated. However, some scholars restrict the application of Matthew 25 to fellow believers, so I chose to focus on a different

passage. See Mark Allan Powell, *God with Us: A Pastoral Theology of Matthew's Gospel* (Minneapolis: Fortress, 1995), and Scot McKnight, *Kingdom Conspiracy: Returning to the Radical Mission of the Local Church* (Grand Rapids, MI: Brazos Press, 2014).

7. The phrase "walk humbly with your God" is notoriously difficult to translate because the word rendered "humbly" is rare in the Bible and its meaning is not entirely clear. Consequently, the final phrase might be more appropriately rendered "walk wisely with God." See James Luther Mays, *Micah: A Commentary*, Old Testament Library (Philadelphia: Westminster Press, 1976), 142.

8. For example, see Joseph A. Fitzmyer, *Romans: A New Translation with Introduction and Commentary*, AB 33 (New York: Doubleday, 1993), 658.

9. See Adam L. Gustine, *Becoming a Just Church: Cultivating Communities of God's Shalom* (Downers Grove, IL: IVP Books, 2019). Gustine seeks to debunk notions of "justice work" as an outreach strategy or as an add-on for interested people. Rather, Christians are to make the pursuit of justice an integral part of discipleship and communal life.

10. Adele Berlin and Marc Zvi Brettler, eds., *The Jewish Study Bible* (Oxford: Oxford University Press, 2004), 899.

CHAPTER 5: THE COMPREHENSIVE GOSPEL

1. See Klyne R. Snodgrass, *You Need a Better Gospel: Reclaiming the Good News of Participation with Christ* (Grand Rapids, MI: Baker Academic, 2022).

2. Mark S. Young, *The Hope of the Gospel: Theological Education and the Next Evangelicalism*, Theological Education between the Times, ed. Ted A. Smith (Grand Rapids, MI: Eerdmans, 2022), 35–42.

3. Scot McKnight, *The King Jesus Gospel: The Original Good News Revisited*, rev. ed. (Grand Rapids, MI: Zondervan, 2016), 28–33.

4. "I'm Just a Bill," from season four of *Schoolhouse Rock!*, first aired March 27, 1976, on ABC. Music and lyrics by Dave Frishberg.

5. "Conjunction Junction," from season two of *Schoolhouse Rock!*, first aired February 10, 1973, on ABC. Music and lyrics by Bob Dorough.

6. Harold W. Hoehner, *Ephesians: An Exegetical Commentary* (Grand Rapids, MI: Baker Academic, 2002), 351–63.

7. Hoehner, *Ephesians*, 351–63.

8. See Jarvis J. Williams, *One New Man: The Cross and Racial Reconciliation in Pauline Theology* (Nashville: B&H Academic, 2010).

9. McKnight, *King Jesus Gospel*, 28–33.

10. Thomas S. Kidd, *George Whitefield: America's Spiritual Founding Father* (New Haven, CT: Yale University Press, 2014).

11. Peter Y. Choi, *George Whitefield: Evangelist for God and Empire* (Grand Rapids, MI: Eerdmans, 2018), 127–68; Kidd, *George Whitefield*, 97–100, 106–29, 188–90.

12. Kidd, *George Whitefield*, 112.

13. Kenneth P. Minkema, "Jonathan Edwards on Slavery and the Slave Trade," *The William and Mary Quarterly* 54, no. 4 (October 1997): 825–26.

14. Jarvis J. Williams, "Biblical Steps toward Removing the Stain of Racism from the Southern Baptist Convention," in *Removing the Stain of Racism from the Southern Baptist Convention: Diverse African American and White Perspectives*, ed. Jarvis J. Williams and Kevin M. Jones (Nashville: B&H Academic, 2017), 21.

15. Martin Luther King Jr., "Letter from Birmingham Jail," in *Why We Can't Wait* (New York: Signet Classics, 2000), 64–84.

CHAPTER 6: THE POWER OF PROXIMITY

1. Henri Nouwen, *Turn My Mourning into Dancing: Finding Hope during Hard Times*, comp. and ed. Timothy Jones (Nashville: W Publishing, 2001), 9.

2. *Merriam-Webster*, s.v. "compassion, *n.*," accessed April 8, 2022, https://www.merriam-webster.com/dictionary/compassion.

3. *Merriam-Webster*, s.v. "just, *adj.*," accessed April 8, 2022, https://www.merriam-webster.com/dictionary/just.

4. Micah Bournes, "Micah Bournes—Is Justice Worth It? (WorldRelief.Org)," May 8, 2013, https://youtu.be/yZ9ze-LTEno. Shared with permission. For more of Bournes's work, see micahbournes.com.

CHAPTER 7: A CALL FOR A MULTI-ABILITY CHURCH

1. Portions of this chapter were excerpted from Daniel's presentation at "The Whole Good News," a Missio Alliance event in August 2021. Used by permission from Missio Alliance.

2. Nancy L. Eiesland, *The Disabled God: Toward a Liberatory Theology of Disability* (Nashville: Abingdon Press, 1994), 99–100.

3. Kathleen A. Cahalan, *Introducing the Practice of Ministry* (Collegeville, MN: Liturgical Press, 2010), 48.

4. Dr. Seuss, *Horton Hears a Who!* (New York: Random House, 1954), 6.

5. Ray Bakke with Jim Hart, *The Urban Christian: Effective Ministry in Today's Urban World* (Downers Grove, IL: InterVarsity Press, 1987), 63.

6. John Swinton, *Becoming Friends of Time: Disability, Timefullness, and Gentle Discipleship* (Waco, TX: Baylor University Press, 2016), 43.

7. Amanda Leduc, *Disfigured: On Fairy Tales, Disability, and Making Space* (Toronto: Coach House Books, 2003).

8. Victor Hugo, *The Hunchback of Notre-Dame*, trans. Walter J. Cobb (London: Penguin Books, 1965).

9. Kathy Black, *A Healing Homiletic: Preaching and Disability* (Nashville: Abingdon Press, 1996), chap. 1.

10. "The Seven Spheres of Influence—Loren Cunningham," YWAM Podcast Network, February 12, 2016, https://ywampodcast.net/shows /teaching/the-seven-spheres-of-influence-loren-cunningham.

11. Jake Uitti, "Strength in the Blues—An Interview with Cornel West," *The Monarch Review*, September 9, 2012, http://www.themonarch review.org/cornel-west-strength-in-the-blues.

CHAPTER 8: WHAT CAN WE DO?

1. Quoted in Rich Stearns, "Blessed by a Broken Heart," World Vision, updated August 28, 2017, https://www.worldvision.org/hunger -news-stories/blessed-broken-heart.

2. Chris Tomlin, Jesse Reeves, Jonas Myrin, and Matt Redman, "Our God," *Passion: Awakening* © 2010 Survivor Records.

3. Martin Luther King Jr., "Remaining Awake through a Great Revolution" (commencement address, Oberlin College, Oberlin, Ohio, June 1965), https://www2.oberlin.edu/external/EOG/BlackHistoryMonth/MLK /CommAddress.html#:~:text=And%20then%20he%20goes%20 on,awake%20through%20a%20great%20revolution.

4. Desmond Tutu, *God Has a Dream: A Vision of Hope for Our Time* (New York: Image Books, 2003), 49–50.

5. DC Talk, "In the Light," *Jesus Freak* © 1995 ForeFront Records.

6. Howard Thurman, *Meditations of the Heart* (Boston: Beacon Press, 1981), 170.

7. "There is no fear in love. But perfect love drives out fear, because fear has to do with punishment. The one who fears is not made perfect in love" (1 John 4:18).

8. This is a helpful article about the context of this quote and its original setting: Takim Williams, "#InContext: Cornel West," Human Trafficking Institute, February 22, 2017, https://traffickinginstitute.org /incontext-cornel-west.

9. Bradley Jersak, *A More Christlike God: A More Beautiful Gospel* (Pasadena, CA: Plain Truth Ministries, 2015), chap. 3.

10. The movement is called IMBY (In My Backyard) and uses tiny homes in backyards to reimagine life together. Check out imbyhomes.org for more info.

11. For more on these travesties, see Charla Bear, "American Indian Board ing Schools Haunt Many," NPR, May 12, 2008, https://www.npr.org /2008/05/12/16516865/american-indian-boarding-schools-haunt -many and Ian Mosby and Erin Millions, "Canada's Residential Schools Were a Horror," *Scientific American*, August 1, 2021, https://www .scientificamerican.com/article/canadas-residential-schools-were-a-horror.

CHAPTER 9: A PEOPLE OF (GLAD) HOPE

1. While this line from the poem by "An Essay on Man" (Alexander Pope, 1733–34) is most often borrowed for baseball, it works in most sports seasons.

2. Marva Dawn, *Truly the Community: Romans 12 and How to Be the Church* (Grand Rapids, MI: Eerdmans, 1997), ix–x.

3. Beth Felker Jones, *Practicing Christian Doctrine: An Introduction to Thinking and Living Theologically* (Grand Rapids, MI: Baker Academic, 2014), 195.

4. Paul Hertig et al., *Breaking through the Boundaries: Biblical Perspectives on Mission from the Outside In* (Maryknoll, NY: Orbis Books, 2019), 22.

5. Hertig et al., *Breaking through*, 28.

6. I am indebted to Dr. Peter Gallagher, Paul Hertig, and others for this line of thinking.

7. For more on *communitas*, see Alan Hirsch, *The Forgotten Ways: Reactivating the Missional Church* (Grand Rapids, MI: Brazos Press, 2006), 25. Hirsch has also written about *communitas* elsewhere.

CHAPTER 10: GOD WILL WIPE EVERY TEAR FROM THEIR EYES

1. India.Arie, "I Am Not My Hair," *Testimony: Vol. 1, Life & Relationship* © 2006 Motown. For more on India.Arie, see http://soulbird.com.

2. "Were You There," first published in 1899. Public domain.

3. Ray Boltz, "Feel the Nails," *Moments for the Heart* © 1994 Word Records.

4. James H. Cone, *The Cross and the Lynching Tree* (Maryknoll, NY: Orbis Books, 2011), 21–22.

5. As quoted in "'Keep Moving from This Mountain,' Address at Spelman College on 10 April 1960," Stanford's Martin Luther King Jr. Research and Education Institute, accessed July 11, 2022, https://kinginstitute .stanford.edu/king-papers/documents/keep-moving-mountain-address -spelman-college-10-april-1960.

CONTRIBUTORS

Jonathan "Pastah J" Brooks is a lifelong resident of Chicago and currently serves as pastor at Lawndale Christian Community Church. Pastah J is a sought-after speaker, writer, artist, and activist, and the author of *Church Forsaken: Practicing Presence in Neglected Neighborhoods.*

Dennis R. Edwards teaches New Testament at North Park Theological Seminary and has served as an urban church planter for three decades in Brooklyn, Washington, DC, and Minneapolis. He and his wife, Susan, are the parents of four adults and grandparents of five children.

Daniel Aaron Harris is a cerebral palsy native Memphian, artist, author, actor, and activist. As the director and founder of Fallen Walls, he encourages and helps people find their vocation inside their location, regardless of their abilities. His writing includes six children's books, articles, and a play that helps change the narrative of disability.

David Hionides serves as the director of Institutional Research and Educational Systems at Denver Seminary. He has also served at Dallas Theological Seminary and taught at Criswell College and Seminario Telological Hebron. He is the author of *Against Irenaean Theodicy: A Refutation of John Hick's Use of Irenaeus.*

Christiana Rice, an on-the-ground practitioner and visionary voice in the parish church movement, serves as codirector of the Parish Collective. She is a trainer, writer, and convener, helping connect people to be the church in the neighborhood. Christiana is coauthor with Michael Frost of *To Alter Your World: Partnering with God to Rebirth Our Communities.*

Aubrey Sampson is the author of several books including *The Louder Song* and *Known*. She has her master's in Evangelism and Leadership, speaks at ministry events all around the United States, and hosts *The Common Good*, a daily talk show in Chicago.

Danielle Strickland's aggressive compassion has served people firsthand in countries all over the world. From establishing justice departments and church plants to launching global antitrafficking initiatives to creating new initiatives to mobilize people toward transformational spiritual life, Danielle trains, advocates, and inspires people to live differently.

Ben Virgo read classics at University College London, is planting a church in the East End of inner-city London, and is employed as a guide, speaker, and podcast host for Christian Heritage London.

Angie Ward is a teacher and author with over thirty years of ministry-leadership experience. She is the general editor of the Kingdom Conversations series and author of *I Am a Leader: When Women Discover the Joy of Their Calling* (both NavPress). She serves as assistant director of the Doctor of Ministry program at Denver Seminary.

Brandon Washington is the pastor of preaching at The Embassy Church in Denver, Colorado. He is a graduate of Denver Seminary, where he studied systematic theology, apologetics, and ethics. He contributed a chapter to *Urban Apologetics: Restoring Black Dignity with the Gospel*.

Lisa Rodriguez-Watson has served as an urban church planter, as a collegiate minister, and in international ministry. Her heart to see people reconciled to God and to one another has led her to invest her life, family, and ministry in places and people that have often been overlooked by the world. She now serves as the national director of Missio Alliance.

ABOUT KINGDOM CONVERSATIONS

To be a Christian is to be conscious of and responsive to three realities at once: the past, where we see that God has spoken and intervened to bless his people to be a blessing; the future, with confidence that God will involve us in his coming resolution of the world's pain and suffering; and the present, where we live, and move, and have our being.

When we step back to consider the vantage point of our good God, who is the same yesterday, today, and forever, we find our footing and our way of glorifying God in our time.

In the Kingdom Conversations series we dare to consider that any issue, no matter how complex, may be brought into conversation with what we know of God and of history and of one another.

They are "conversations" because they gather the perspectives of various Christian leaders to consider the question together.

They are "Kingdom" because they are each submitted in humility and hope to God, trusting that God himself will lead us into all truth.